DARE TO
DREAM

The Story of L'Bri Pure n' Natural

LINDA & BRIAN KAMINSKI
With Jim Waldsmith

CEDAR HILL PUBLISHING

Dare to Dream: The story of L'Bri Pure n' Natural

Photo on page 117 by Barbara J. Slane

Editing by Rebecca Hayes

Book and cover design by Rebecca Hayes

Published in the United States by
Cedar Hill Publishing
www.cedarhillpublishing.com

ISBN-10: 1-933324-75-9
ISBN-13: 978-1-933324-75-3

Library of Congress Control Number 2007922808

DEDICATION

To all those among us possessing dreams for a better life. With courage and determination, may you dispel the doubters, overcome discouragement, and gain confidence in your quest for success.

LINDA & BRIAN KAMINSKI

THE BUTTERFLY

Throughout the world, the gentle butterfly symbolizes the joy of life, the desire for happiness, and the search for beauty. When a butterfly opens and stretches its wings for the first time, and then takes flight, it's a miraculous moment.

TABLE OF CONTENTS

PREFACE

"Only famous people write books about themselves." This is what Linda and Brian Kaminski told me when I met with them during the summer of 2006. We were in the corporate offices of L'Bri Pure n' Natural. (A combination of Linda and Brian, pronounced Lih-Brye.) As a writer, I was telling them they had a good story to tell, a story about real people who built an amazing business based on honesty, integrity, and doing the right things. "It just doesn't sit well," Brian protested. "A book about us?"

"Oh, we could write a book all right," Linda chimed in with a laugh, "All the things we've seen? But please, we don't live in the past. There's so much more to get done."

Despite their reservations, I hooked up a tape recorder and began asking questions – and listening. This is Linda and Brian's story – a story that will inspire you, perhaps amaze you, and certainly will give you hope that, in this world of Wall Street scandals and Washington insiders, there are still people like the Kaminskis, quietly making a difference and doing good things for so many others.

JIM WALDSMITH,
March 2007

INTRODUCTION

At first glance, L'Bri Pure n' Natural is anything but extraordinary. Sure, it's a multi-million-dollar company. Customers by the tens of thousands rave about their products. Those who work there and work with the owners, from vendors to Consultants to customers, are quick to laud Linda and Brian's integrity.

Located in a modest industrial park on the outskirts of Mukwonago, Wisconsin, thirty minutes in good traffic from Milwaukee, the corporate offices of L'Bri Pure n' Natural is humming with activity.

This year, the company will ship more than 200,000 bottles and jars of skin care lotion, face and body scrub, diet supplements, beauty enhancers, and other products direct to customers.

Also this year, the company will mail commission checks approaching a million dollars to its independent sales force of L'Bri Consultants.

In and of themselves, these facts, albeit impressive, are far from extraordinary. But first glances can be deceiving. In the history of American business, L'Bri Pure n' Natural is extraordinary due to the work ethic and faith of two people – Linda and Brian Kaminski.

The daughter of immigrants and the son of a father born in poverty, Linda and Brian put everything on the line. They invested their savings, mortgaged their home, sold their car, borrowed on credit cards, and when that fell short, sold many of their possessions to raise money to start their business. Without a car, Brian pedaled a bicycle about town, while Linda gave away samples of their skin care lotion to customers in a Wal-Mart parking lot. One customer at a time, they dared to dream, and along the way built an American success story.

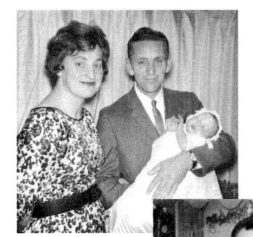

*Philipp and
Gertrude Roth with
Linda's brother,
Karl.*

*Tony & Dolores
Kaminski*

1: FAMILY

Linda with her parents, left, and Brian's baby picture

Together From The Start

Linda and Brian have been together practically from day one. And that is not an exaggeration. They were born two days apart, on January 6 and January 8 in 1957 at the same hospital – Milwaukee's St. Joseph on West Chambers Street. Brian's mother delivered first, and Linda's mom followed suit two days later. As Brian tells the story, "In those days, of course, babies were in the nursery for at least a week. So we were obviously in the same baby room at the same time."

Whenever Brian talks about this amazing coincidence, Linda invariably chimes in with a laugh, "I never had a chance."

Years later, Linda's mother recalled seeing a vivacious lady who was also a new mother in St. Joseph Hospital that week. "That was my mom," Brian completes the tale with a knowing smile. "I don't know if I buy that or not, but oh well, that's what Linda's mother says."

Coming Of Age In A Chaotic Time

Linda's family history runs deep in the picture-postcard region of Bavaria where the Danube, Inn, and Ilz rivers converge at the town of Passau. Today, tourists enjoy seeing the Fortress of Oberhaus, built in 1219 on the wooded cliffs overlooking the Rhine, photographing the stately castles, and walking the bridges of this ancient city that dates to the time of the Roman Legion.

However, in the mid-1930s, with the Nazi Party coming to power, this community near the Austrian border some ninety miles from Munich was torn in its loyalties. Germany, defeated in the first World War, its economy impoverished by the global depression, was close to collapse. Adolph Hitler assumed the office of Reich President, abolished the justice system, imposed censorship, and began the systematic elimination of Jews, Gypsies, Slavs, and others the Nazis deemed "undesirable." Hitler called for massive re-armament and the conscription of soldiers into a new and powerful military. Austria was taken over by the German army, but many Austrians remained fiercely independent and anti-Nazi.

In this time of political turmoil and uncertainty, Linda's mother, Gertrude Klessinger, came of age. The Klessingers, in defiance of the Nazis, participated in an underground effort to smuggle Jews, Poles, and others into Austria. "They hid people in their little apartment," Linda says, "until it was safe to take them into Austria." Unknown to her own mother, Gertrude did more than hide refugees. In the cover of darkness, she personally led them across the border. "There were all kinds of people the Germans wanted to eliminate," Linda says. "When I went back to visit with my mom at the age of almost 16, she actually took me on the route she used as a child to lead people across into Austria.

"And it was difficult, because it's very hilly and

maybe not mountains, per se, but close to it." Linda describes the geography on the rugged Austrian border: "You're climbing these steep, mountainous hills, crawling through cattle wire and things like that.

"I actually visited the bomb shelter she ran to as a child when they had to escape the bombs. It was an eerie feeling to walk in there. There was a presence, a feeling of foreboding and fear. You could imagine these people huddled together in terror."

Linda's mother told her of the time she secretly slipped out of the house to escort a family across the border. "My mother was thirteen years of age, and the escaping family did not have the proper papers and documents to leave the country legally, so the only way out of Germany was to flee across the border at night," Linda explains. After delivering the family into friendly hands in Austria, the teenaged Gertrude was working her way back home through the darkened streets when a policeman stopped her. She knew that to be exposed helping fugitives was a crime that meant imprisonment, if not death. The suspicious officer asked her business. "I was at my boyfriend's house and am now on my way home," Gertrude responded. "Why doesn't your boyfriend escort you to your house?" the officer queried, looking into the youngster's eyes to catch her in a lie. That was when the quick-thinking Gertrude told the officer her boyfriend was very ill and there was disease in the house. The officer, fearful for his own safety, told Gertrude to hurry home, alone.

On one of the most harrowing journeys into Austria, Gertrude guided a woman and her two young children through the rocky terrain in the black of night. The woman's husband had been killed, and she had nothing left. Safely into Austria, the woman pressed a ring into Gertrude's tiny hand. "I want you to have this. You saved my family's life this night."

Linda pauses and quietly adds, "My mother had that

ring for many years and treasures that memory. Later, she gave the ring to me."

As the war drew to an end, food was scarce, and the family was often hungry. "She told me stories about how food was just so hard to find," Linda recalls, "that half the time, she found herself lightheaded and would literally pass out."

A Teenager On The Russian Front

While Gertrude and her family struggled to survive, the man who would become Linda's father was also growing up in Germany. His name: Philipp Roth. Explains Linda, "My dad was very entrepreneurial. He was pretty much on his own by the time he was fourteen. He came from a big family of five children, and it was a very wealthy family, but when the war broke out, everything was taken away – their land, their home. He actually was in Yugoslavia when they changed the borders, so they lost everything."

Drafted into the German army, Philipp was sent to the Russian Front. He was not yet fifteen years of age. Captured by the Russians, he was in a Soviet prison camp. Linda says her father related the story of his harrowing escape with the help of a Polish girl named Pianka. "Thank goodness, I didn't get that name," Linda laughs now when retelling the story. "Dad was shot in the leg during the escape, and the Polish girl came to his rescue, keeping him safe in their horse stall. She hid him under the hay and nursed him until his leg was well enough so he could walk again."

Philipp returned to the German army, but the teenager was again captured, this time by the Poles fighting alongside the Russians. Assigned to a slave labor work gang, he was repairing railroad tracks when he and a Gypsy overpowered two Polish guards and escaped into the woods. Linda picks up the story, "They were on the run and saw a number of soldiers. They may have been Americans, but I'm not sure. My dad thought this was the end, because they were surrounded. And then one of the soldiers walked up to them and said, 'It's over. The war is over.'"

At war's end, young Philipp Roth searched for his family and learned they had been relocated to Passau. He traveled to the Bavarian town and happily found members of his family alive. It was about this time he was befriended by the Klessingers. Gertrude's father died during the war, and her mother took in the former soldier and treated him as a son. "My dad lived with my mother's family and helped care for my grandmother," Linda relates. "He helped out with my grandmother's three children and was like another son to her." The lovely Gertrude, at five feet nine inches, considered tall for her age, with long, dark chestnut hair, alabaster skin, and exquisite green eyes did not go unnoticed. Philipp was soon in love. So was Gertrude. After all, the thin, muscular Philipp was over six feet tall, had the chiseled features of a movie idol, luxurious, dark hair, and piercing blue eyes that were unforgettable.

"But his dream was to come to America," Linda says. "So at the age of twenty-one, he came here on his own, and my mother stayed in Germany."

It was December 1952 when Philipp boarded a ship for the voyage to New York. Arriving in America, the young man marveled at the sight of Manhattan Island, bedecked in Christmas finery, holiday lights ablaze by the millions, and storefronts loaded with merchandise. Making his way to Pennsylvania Station, he purchased a ticket to Chicago and from there, on to Milwaukee, a city settled by German immigrants and proud of its Teutonic heritage.

Less than twenty-four hours after departing Manhattan, the train pulled into Milwaukee. Philipp was immediately employed by the Grede Foundry, the firm that sponsored his passage to the United States. In the months to come, a portion of his paycheck was used to repay the company.

Together At Last, In America

Determined to succeed in this land of the free, Philipp devoted every spare moment to learn the language of his adopted country and saved every penny to earn passage to bring Gertrude to America. Fourteen months later, he had the cash in hand, and the ticket was purchased.

It was a grand day of tears and laughter when, at age twenty-one, Gertrude finally arrived in Milwaukee to start this exciting new life. Soon, she was employed as well, working as a laborer at the downtown Milwaukee Gallun & Sons leather factory. Phillip could not afford an automobile, but he had a motorcycle. "That's how they would go to work – on a motorcycle," Linda says with a smile.

For the young couple, America was the Promised Land. "They came here and drooled," Linda says. "There was so much abundance, food everywhere, warm clothing, shoes, everything you could ever want."

Gertrude and Philipp were married on a cold January day in 1953, and a picture was made to preserve the moment. The bride wore a navy blue dress and carried red roses, the groom's favorite. "They had a party at The Bavarian Inn," Linda says. "It was very simple. A lot of food and dancing, but they didn't go on a honeymoon, because there was no money for a wedding trip."

It was traditional for friends to give the newlyweds money. With this cash as a start, Philipp and Gertrude frugally saved a little each week from their earnings until, two years later, they could purchase their first automobile, a Chrysler DeSoto.

"For my dad, because of what he went through in

Germany, America was always known as the 'land of opportunity.' It's what everybody talked about – getting to America." According to Linda, her father's "big dream" was to own a German-style restaurant. "He was a fabulous cook," Linda says.

Philipp worked as a laborer on various construction projects. In 1954, he was a foreman during the construction of the 45-acre Bayshore Shopping Center in Glendale, Wisconsin. The strenuous work aggravated the leg injury suffered during the war, and the pain in his leg became a chronic problem. He took a job as a machinist and later studied to become a crane operator, eventually landing a job at D.G. Beyer Company, a pioneer in the use of truck-mounted hydraulic cranes.

The young couple eventually settled in an apartment off Roosevelt Drive. He never opened the restaurant of his dreams, but Philipp became one of Milwaukee's best crane operators, responsible for lifting the steel for a number of the city's tallest and largest buildings. He helped build the graceful Hoan Memorial Bridge that crosses the Milwaukee River at Lake Michigan. During the mammoth construction project, he fell into the river and survived, no worse for wear.

"My dad was always one who said he loved coming to America," Linda recalls with a warm smile. "He wanted to escape everything that happened in Europe, because it was so horrific. I don't think he ever regretted coming here. He didn't have the advantage of a topnotch education, so I think, for what they came here with, which was nothing, what they accomplished is amazing. My parents really are an American success story. They prove that in this land of opportunity, for the people who come here, work hard and have a dream, anything is possible."

Laughter, Good Food, And Fun

The home was filled with laughter and good food. Gertrude provided the laughter. "Mom was very fun-loving," Linda says. "She was always the one telling the jokes." Linda's dad was the great cook, preparing traditional German fare – pfannekuchen (potato pancakes); krautsalat (hot cabbage salad); wurstsalat (sausage salad); sauerbraten; and his favorite dish, satrash, a Yugoslavian cabbage and meat stew.

"My brother, Karl, and I grew up in a very German home," Linda continues. "Every weekend was the German Club. The German Club was all about getting together and partying with German people. There would be German dancing. There would be Halloween parties and Maifest, which is where you climb the pole and get the gifts down for your children. Dad and the other fathers would climb this huge pole and whatever they could grab, they threw down to their kids. That's a special spring celebration. A lot of bratwurst, lots of sauerkraut, sauerbraten, and, of course, a lot of beer."

Linda learns to polka in the arms of her father at a gathering of Milwaukee's German Club.

The German community eventually pooled their resources and purchased land for a German park near Grafton, Wisconsin. River Park was a lush wooded setting and in the center, the traditional hofbrauhaus, complete with deer antlers and a collection of authentic beer steins. As members of the park, the family was entitled to construct their own get-away cottage. "They leased a little parcel of land in the park, and then dad built the cottage. It was a very humble cottage," Linda remembers, "but he built it, it was his cottage, and it still stands today."

Linda describes her mother as "very loving, very generous" but admits, "my father was the person that influenced me the most. My father was really the person that I looked up to. Dad was always positive and, for the most part, encouraged me."

From both parents, she inherited the belief in the value of hard work. "Growing up, I developed a desire to not have to struggle in life, but I knew in order to get things you wanted, there was a price to pay. You have to have a really strong desire, and you have to really want what you want, and you have to really *know* what you want."

Philipp and Gertrude knew what they wanted, and they worked hard to get it. Linda's mother never learned to drive a car, but during most of Linda's youth, she brought home a paycheck, initially from the leather factory and later from the sprawling Briggs & Stratton plant. "I remember when I was little," Linda says, "my dad bundled me up, and we took the DeSoto to pick up mom from work. She worked the second shift, getting off at midnight. Usually I fell asleep on the back seat." Gertrude worked second shift at Briggs & Stratton for nearly twenty years.

Always The Optimist

Philipp Roth was a survivor, and perhaps because of his harrowing experiences in the World War, an optimist who always saw the silver lining. "My dad was the visionary of the family. He would be the one who would say,

'There are going to be some challenges,' but he saw the big picture in everything. Where somebody else would say, 'You're crazy. Look at what you're risking here,' my dad somehow always saw beyond that, and that's probably what I think I picked up the most from him. You know there will be obstacles, but you'll get through them. Somehow you'll find a way, and everything will be okay in the end.

"He believed in goodness and nature and the Golden Rule," Linda says. "He always said, 'Why does it always have to be so complicated? You know, it can be so simple. It could be so easy.' He loved nature and felt that God was pretty much everywhere. On his deathbed, he told me, 'You'll find me in nature.'"

Learning The Ways Of The Old Country

Even though German was spoken in the home much of the time, both parents learned English and were proud when they became United States citizens. Despite their Americanization, they insisted Linda learn the ways of the old country. On Saturday mornings, she attended German language and culture classes at a German-operated school located in downtown Milwaukee on Fond du Lac Avenue. Today, Linda speaks and writes fluent German as a second language.

This came in handy when Linda began dating young Brian Kaminski. In the lad's presence, Gertrude and Linda talked about him – in German! "I didn't have any idea what they were saying about me," Brian recalls with a note of exasperation. Says Linda, "We used to do it – well, we did that just to annoy him. We kind of ganged up on Brian a bit, you know, because he's the Polish one in the family."

Tony Kaminski, left, with Dr. Bartlett Joshua Palmer, president of the Palmer School of Chiropractic, Davenport, Iowa.

Tony's diploma from the Palmer School of Chiropractic, received July 20, 1954. This diploma was proudly displayed at his office throughout his years of practice.

Setting Sights On A Better Life

Drive due west on State Route 73, a little more than 100 miles northwest of Milwaukee as the crow flies, you find the village of Plainfield. Blink your eyes, and you might miss the ten streets that meet or cross the highway at this junction in Wisconsin's Waushara County. Life can be tough in places like Plainfield, and living was mighty tough there during the 1930s Great Depression.

The Kaminski family of seven children was considered poor, even by Plainfield standards. Relying on government assistance, they stretched the meager food they had and made do. When Brian's father, Tony, marked his seventeenth birthday, he turned his back on Plainfield and headed out of town on State Route 73, his sights set on

Milwaukee and a better life. He was determined to make something of himself, maybe become a doctor, and never want for anything again.

In the mid-1950s, Milwaukee was renowned for its beer, and one of the largest breweries in town was Schlitz. Tony landed an entry-level job at Schlitz Beer, located a room, and was off and running. Soon he had a second job, in addition to working at Schlitz. Says Brian, "Dad would work a couple of jobs, and he would sleep on the bus between the two jobs. He was motivated to get ahead."

Determined to become a doctor, Tony applied to the famed Palmer School of Chiropractic in Davenport, Iowa. In the early to mid-1950s, Palmer was already the acclaimed "birthplace" of chiropractic, having been founded by D.D. Palmer in 1897. His son, Dr. B.J. Palmer, was now the school's president and a leading authority in treatment based on spinal realignment. His methods were considered controversial and often frowned upon by the medical profession, but there were many adherents to the use of chiropractic methods for treating a number of conditions and ailments. As Tony studied at Palmer, he likely was engrained with a number of B.J. Palmer's "epigrams," including this one: "Throw away your wishbone, straighten up your backbone, stick out your jawbone, and go for it."

Growing Up In The "Leave It To Beaver" Home

With his hard-won degree in hand, in 1954 Tony returned to Milwaukee, a doctor at last. "To come from such a poor family and achieve his dream, to become a chiropractor, was a huge success for him and his family," Brian relates. "He was very proud."

Opening his practice in Milwaukee, Tony earned extra income selling Nutri-lite vitamins and other supplements through direct sales. A few years later, Jay Van Andel and Richard DeVos, two Michigan entrepreneurs, purchased the Nutri-lite company and launched Amway. It was at a Nutri-lite distributor meeting that Tony took note of an attractive young woman.

Brian, age 3, with his parents, Tony and Dolores Kaminski

Dolores Kuchenreuther was an effervescent, outgoing, petite woman who dreamed of someday becoming a dancer like Ginger Rogers or Vera-Ellen. She dyed her hair platinum blonde to accent her delicate features, round face, and blue eyes. Dolores always wore stylish clothes, shoes, and accessories. Standing next to Tony, at 160 pounds on a muscular five-foot-eight-inch frame, they made a striking couple. They married in 1955 and decided to try a new life in Saskatchewan, Canada, but within a year moved back to Milwaukee and purchased a house. The next winter, Dolores gave birth to Brian.

"I was raised in the 'Leave It To Beaver' family," Brian says. "I was an only child. It was a perfect family home, every part of it. I have great memories of Mom's cooking, and my dad working. They were happy, and I can see him cutting the grass. It was just the perfect childhood.

"Their first home had the chiropractic office in the house. He carried that through his whole career. He always had his practice in the home. Granted, he built on a little addition to the house, but he was always working out of the home."

Dr. Tony Kaminski treated a list of on-going clients, including several Milwaukee notables – a well-known radio personality and several elected officials.

"As a chiropractor, my dad was very health conscious and always talked about positive thinking," Brian recalls. "So I was brought up very health conscious, with good nutrition, vitamin supplements, drink lots of water, do the right things. I never had an inoculation in my life, which was unusual. At the time, it was a challenge for them to keep me from getting the typical shots, such as tetanus. In fact, my first needle poke was for the blood test before we got married, and I almost passed out."

The Kaminskis studied many religions, Brian says. "My parents exposed me to all different religions and when I was in grade school, they sent me to a class led by a lady named June, who was almost like a psychiatrist-type person. She taught children how to work their minds and think good thoughts.

"At about age seven, they made me go to tap dancing school, which I didn't like at all. I studied tap for ten years." Thinking back on his childhood, Brian believes his mother, who wanted to be a dancer, encouraged him to have the career she never had.

The pinnacle of Brian's dancing career came when he was cast as a child-performer in a production of the musical "Camelot," starring Robert Goulet at Milwaukee's Pabst Theater. "It was a big deal at the time," he laughs, recalling the memories. "I was a page boy in the play. I had been taking tap dancing for five years by that time. My mom did a little ballet when she was younger. Mom and Dad liked the idea of dance in general, just for coordination, and there were acrobatics, somersaults, and gymnastics. But I disliked it tremendously, the whole time."

Despite his dislike for dance, Brian continued the lessons, until he met Linda. Linda recalls what happened: "I was dating Brian, and I didn't know he was a tap dancer. One day, a girl came up to me and said, 'Oh, you're Brian Kaminski's girlfriend; I'm his dance partner.' And I looked at her. Out of the blue. All I knew was that on Thursday nights, we could never talk or do anything. Thursday nights, this guy was just not available, and I never questioned it.

"When I found out he was in dance school, I thought it was kind of neat and told him so. That's when he told his parents, 'I'm done.'"

"I had been trying to get out of it forever," Brian says. "I guess there were a couple of good things that came out of that experience. I got to be in front of people, be on stage, and do shows. We traveled to retirement communities and put on shows and recitals. And I learned to ride a unicycle, which I think is one of the cooler things." Brian continues to ride a unicycle and in recent years, taught their son, Andy, to ride one, too.

Living The Simple Life

"Growing up was great," Brian says. "It was very simple. There weren't a lot of things, because dad made just enough money to live a simple life. And that was okay. We didn't go on vacations, but we rented a boat, and my dad and I went fishing. Later, we golfed together quite a bit. There were pick-up baseball and football games with the kids in the neighborhood. I had lots of friends and when I was old enough for Cub Scouts, my mom was the den leader. Since mom loved dance and studied ballet as a youngster, she had our den do the 'Can-Can' at one of the scout meetings. Here we are, all these boys dressed up, and we're kicking our legs. Funny thing, I don't remember it being a problem for anyone."

Thinking back, Brian says, "I always said I was spoiled, not so much with stuff, but with attention and love."

In the winter, Brian shoveled driveways for spending money and in the summer, mowed grass. He sold seed packets, door-to-door, in the spring and raked leaves in the fall.

Every summer, Brian spent two weeks on a farm located outside of Plainfield. "My dad's sister had a farm, so I went up there, which was a super experience, working, having fun, doing a little hunting and fishing.

"I became very independent by the time I learned to drive, at about age sixteen," Brian recalls. "I was away from home all the time, working to earn money to buy a car. When I was home, I lived in the basement, where I made up my own little apartment. I cooked my meals and washed my own clothes."

*Linda & Brian began dating in the ninth grade.
Here they are at age 16.*

2: Linda and Brian

Meeting For A Second Time

Brian and his family resided in suburban Milwaukee, near the corner of Fond du Lac and 60th Street. Unknown to the young Brian, Linda's home was just over a mile away, due west, at Capitol and North 71st Street. They met for the second time (remember St. Joseph Hospital?) in high school in the ninth grade.

In Northwest Milwaukee, about midway between the Kaminski home and the Roth house stands John Marshall High School, a sprawling campus of four massive buildings, each the length of a city block. It was here that ninth graders Brian and Linda joined the Class of 1975.

"High school was a whole new world," Linda remembers. "There's a whole other breed of people there, from all walks of life. I never got into the bad crowd, but I was not one that earned the best grades, either. I would sleep in poetry class, for example. My poetry teacher would be up there with 'Annabel Lee,' that poem, and there's Linda falling asleep. He was boring. He had no sense of humor. He would tell my parents, 'She sleeps in my class.' I could not keep my eyes open to save my life." Edgar Allan Poe may have been a challenge, but Linda excelled in typing, shorthand, and English grammar.

They were fifteen years old and new to the ninth grade. Always confident, perhaps due to his years on stage in tap shoes, Brian boldly invited Linda to the Walgreen's Drug Store at Capitol Court Shopping Center for hotdogs. "I thought he was really cute," Linda explains. "He had this real thick, chestnut brown, curly hair." They were getting along well, until Brian clumsily knocked over his glass of milk, spilling the white liquid across the counter and into Linda's lap.

"I don't know if he was clumsy or nervous or what it was," Linda says.

"All of the above," Brian grimaces. "From then on,

every time we went out, I made a mess."

Linda explains: "It was crazy. It was so funny, because every time we were together, something would spill. If it wasn't the water glass, it was something else. One time, he was drinking root beer. He started choking on the root beer, and this was one of the first few dates we had. So I started to wonder about him, and I'm thinking, 'What's with this guy? He's always spilling something.' But that worked its way out, eventually."

But Is He German?

Linda was willing to overlook the spills, but her parents were not pleased. When she introduced her new boyfriend to mom and dad Roth, Linda remembers, "My mom thought he was cute, but the first question, of course, was, 'Is he German?' I said, 'No, he's Polish, but that's close, you know, this close.' My Mom didn't think it was going to amount to much at the time, but then when she saw that we were on the phone more and all I talked about was Brian, she discouraged me and tried to lead me back to German boys.

"My parents always wanted me to marry a German," Linda says. "From early on, the intent was for me to marry a German boy, because the German culture was very important to my parents. They wanted to keep that German bloodline going."

To please her parents, Linda dated a few other boys, all from German stock. One German father was so taken with Linda, he promised if she would marry his son, he would buy the newlyweds a house. "I was literally bribed by the boy's family," Linda says, adding, "But I liked Brian best. When I met him, something just felt right. You know, when you meet people, sometimes you feel a chemistry? There's a connection. And that's something I felt, and I also liked his personality. He had an aura about him that was very self-assured. He was his own person. So many of the guys I knew back then were such followers. Brian didn't really fit into the average mold of the guys I knew.

"In high school we dated other people, and then would be together again. We would break up, and I would date someone else. I dated the captain of the football team for a while, and then I dated the top hippy of the school. He wore one of those big jackets, decorated with fringe. He let me wear his purple jacket, which was a real big thing.

"Somehow, I was always drawn back to Brian. Even when I was dating other people, he was never completely out of my head. It was his personality. He had an air of confidence. You could see he was comfortable in his own skin. He wasn't trying to be anybody else. Other guys were always playing games, and they weren't real. He was just a real cut-and-dried, down-to-earth person."

Find A Good German Boy

Philipp and Gertrude Roth let their daughter know they did not approve of Brian Kaminski. "It's not that they didn't like him for any character traits," Linda continues. "It was just because he wasn't German. They tried to stop me from seeing him, but when they saw how unhappy I was and that we really clicked when we were together, they began to warm up to him.

"My parents thought we were too young, and there was some truth to that, but I think sometimes you do know who is right for you. And to think that we were born in the same hospital, two days apart, I think sometimes there is a plan or a reason for things to happen the way they do.

"I dated other boys, and they didn't spill things on me," she laughs. "But there wasn't that feeling I had when I was with Brian. Brian is a lot like my dad, and they do sometimes say that you marry your father. And as he's matured, he's gotten more and more like my dad. So I probably had that sense already, when I met him."

By the time Brian was sixteen and able to drive, he started buying, fixing up, racing, and selling cars to buy more cars. "These were beaters, one-hundred dollar cars," he says. There was a Charger and a Riviera, a Chevy and a Chrysler. "I would buy a car every three months, work on the engine, race it, and then sell it and get another. I probably had twenty-five to thirty cars.

"I got into racing," he explains. "I souped them up, and we went drag racing. Linda came along. I did that as a hobby for quite a few years."

By the tenth grade, Brian lost all interest in formal education. "I skipped out a lot, so I wasn't at school much. I was too busy driving my car, working on it. I wasn't very interested in school at all, so it's my fault Linda's grades might have slipped," Brian admits.

Linda's mother often walked to the neighborhood shopping center, Capitol Court. To walk to Capitol Court, she needed to pass by the high school and on these particular days, she invariably commented to Linda, "I saw Brian driving around the school today."

"That was what the kids did back then," Linda says. "If you had a car, you cruised around the school, and kids hopped in and out of your car. There may be two cars circling the school, everybody else was in class. There were two cars, and one of them, of course, would be Brian's car. But we thought we were cool when we were doing it. Driving, listening to the radio. We just thought that was the neatest thing. My mother didn't like it, and she didn't like the fact that I wasn't interested in school anymore."

Linda Lands A Job

Linda was fifteen when she received a worker's permit "I worked my first job at Arthur Treacher's Fish & Chips," she says, "and I did a lot of babysitting."

Linda worked as a clerk at a local cosmetics store, Pill n' Puff, and later applied for a position in the bakery department of Kohl's, a large supermarket. "Herbert Kohl, who later became our U.S. Senator, interviewed me for my job in the bakery," Linda says. "He asked me, 'If apples sell for $1.29 a dozen, how much is one apple? I'm not good with numbers. I don't know how I passed that interview. Somehow my brain kicked in, and I got it right. I got the job." From then on, Linda always had a job and at every job, she excelled and earned promotions.

Through their high school years, Linda and Brian went to drive-in movies, enjoyed roller skating, or checked out a dance at St. Pius Church. "We went to my house," Brian says. "We would go to the basement, to my mini-apartment, and watch TV. We just spent a lot of time getting to know one another."

We're Going To The Prom

It was time for the senior prom. Admits Brian, "We were not into proms, but it was a convenient excuse to go on a special date."

Adds Linda, "Plus, it was a way to get money to go to a fancy restaurant to eat."

Linda selected a prom gown, but they had no intention of attending the dance. Brian recalls, "I had just gotten another 'new-to-me car,' a 1950 Chevy, and at that time, that was a real old car."

"He picked me up in this car for the prom, and my mother about had a heart attack," Linda relates what happened. "Here I am with this beautiful white dress that mom

Brian & Linda on Prom Night

spent a lot of money on, and here he comes with this 1950 jalopy!"

"This is in 1975, and I come up in a 1950 Chevy, which is not a neat antique at that time. "Rusted out fenders, stick shift on the steering wheel and that beige fuzzy kind of interior," Brian describes their ride for this once-in-a-lifetime evening. They dined at one of Milwaukee's most exclusive restaurants, Jean Paul. The meal was delicious. Back in the car, Brian was a bit heavy on the gas, and a police cruiser pulled in behind them.

"And we got a ticket!" Linda exclaims. "What would Mother have thought of that?"

Divorce "Leave It To Beaver" Style

As graduation day approached, Brian received the shock of his young life. His parents announced intentions to separate and divorce. "Until then, I had no idea they were unhappy with one another. Supposedly, they made sure they stuck together until I was eighteen."

In the years leading to the divorce, with Brian situated in high school, Dolores enrolled in beautician school and became a hairdresser. In retrospect, Brian says his father may not have supported the idea of his wife working outside the home. "He liked the 'Leave it to Beaver' lifestyle.   Nothing wrong with that, of course, but Mom wanted to do more things. So she kind of left the nest."

After the divorce, Dolores operated a beauty shop, became interested in yoga, and remarried. Linda offers her perspective: "Dolores was such a good mother for so many years, and when Brian was out on his own, she wanted to spread her wings. She experienced a difficult childhood. Her mother passed away when she was seven years old, from cancer.   Within a month, her father, heartbroken, wrote a suicide note, saying he couldn't live without her, and gassed himself to death in the kitchen. After the funeral, the children were sent to an orphanage. Later, the father's sister took in the three young children." The sister did not have children of her own. Says Brian softly, "They lived on a farm. It was a very tough life. My mother and her two brothers say they were never very happy in that household."

Linda & Brian at age 18: They completed high school in 1975.

Two Credits Short

The Kaminski family was breaking up, and Brian, never a very good student, wanted to get out of high school as quickly as possible. However, he was two credits shy of the number required to graduate. He made an appointment with the vice principal, Mr. Jankowski, to plead his case. "I remember going to his office and telling him some story. I don't know what it was. I was working at a gas station and had two jobs," Brian remembers. "I was out working and making money to buy a car and get an apartment. We talked, and under the table, the vice-principal gave me two credits. And so, boom, I'm free to go. I had no interest in college, even though my Dad had gone to college. I just wanted to get out there and start making three dollars an hour and get into the game of life."

Linda, Wisconsin Needs You

In her senior year of high school, Linda was earning passing grades, but excelled in secretarial courses such as typing and shorthand. At this time, the lieutenant governor of Wisconsin, Martin J. "Marty" Schreiber, put together one of the nation's first nursing home residents' ombudsman programs. A staunch advocate for the elderly, Schreiber wanted to give nursing home residents a voice and a means to register complaints. Working with a slim budget, the program's administrator, Mandy Zubatsky, requested the secretarial program at Marshall High School refer a few of their most promising students to work on the project. Eleven Marshall senior students were sent to Miss Zubatsky for interviews. She was to select one. Linda Roth was on the list.

"They were looking for someone to accompany the investigators on these complaints," Linda explains. "I would travel right along with the investigator and take notes. I was good in shorthand, but I wasn't the best by any means.

"I went to the interview with the other girls, but I really in no way thought I was going to get this job. There were girls on this interview who were so much better in school than I was, but I thought, I'll go for the experience of having a job interview."

Two weeks passed, and Linda says she forgot all about the ombudsman program, Mandy Zubatsky, and the job interview. "All of sudden, I get a phone call, and it's Miss Zubatsky, and she says, 'I've made my decision, and I'd like you to come for a second interview.' I did, and I got the job.

"I was stunned. I was really amazed. After a few months on the job, I finally asked her, 'You know, I wasn't the best candidate. I wasn't the fastest. Why did you hire me?' And she said, 'Of all the girls, your people skills were the best and your handshake. You were the only one who had a firm handshake.' That's what got the job for me. It was not that I was the speediest, but it had something to do with my people skills. So that taught me something."

A few weeks after graduation, Linda Roth, at age 18, became an employee of the State of Wisconsin, working with the lieutenant governor on a groundbreaking effort to help her state's nursing home residents. In the months to follow, she met with Marty Schreiber, traveled to the state capitol in Madison, dined in the homes of top government administrators, and received increased responsibility.

"I started mixing with a different quality of people. They were educated, refined, and I really enjoyed some of the homes that I was in, and I'm thinking, 'Wow, this is how the other part of the world lives.'"

The lovely homes, extravagant dinners, and high-level meetings were fun and exciting, but Linda soon discovered a darker side to her work. The visits to nursing homes were like stepping into another world. "What I saw happening to the elderly we visited was very emotional for me," she says. "I had nightmares. I couldn't sleep at night. It was horrible."

To this day, the memories are difficult to handle. "The bed sores, understaffing, drugging of retarded female patients so the older men could have sex with them, giving these helpless women birth control pills so they wouldn't get pregnant. We had women in the nursing homes that were mentally retarded that were getting pregnant. To see these people so mistreated. There was no respect for humanity. None.

"One time, I was with the investigator while the aides handed out food trays," Linda describes a fairly typical observation. "I waited in the corridor while the investigator talked to the administrator about a complaint, and one of the women sat in a wheelchair, adjacent to the door. The aide plopped the tray down, and the patient said, 'Oh, I have to go to the bathroom really bad. Can you help me?' And the aide said, 'I got to get these trays out before they get cold. I'll be back in a little bit.' Well, twenty-five minutes later, I'm still sitting there, and the lady soiled herself. When the aide returned, she was very mean to her. She roughly yanked her out of the chair and said, 'You're going to have to eat this cold stuff. I'm not happy about cleaning your mess.' The woman, embarrassed, cried, and I told the investigator there was another complaint.

"No one should be treated that way. It was awful, and I'd go home at night, so affected by it all," Linda remembers. "You have to have a real tough hide to do a job like that, and I don't have that. Your heart goes out to those people, and I had nightmares. I had stomach pain."

Higher Expectations

Not yet nineteen years old, Linda developed stomach ulcers. After nine months in the ombudsman program, she turned in her two-week notice. "They begged me not to leave, and I said, 'I just can't. This job is so depressing.'"

So ended Linda's first "real" job, and the experience,

both bad and good, stayed with her. The horrors of the nursing homes faded over the years, but the positive aspects of this important work provided a lifetime of inspiration. "From watching Mandy Zubatsky, I saw a woman in her early thirties, self-assured, possessing high expectations for herself and the others around her, and with a great sense of humor. She was a different class of person altogether. I can't say she was my first mentor, but she was the woman that made me see there are more things in life. That I should have high expectations for myself. That I could do more and be more. She was the first person who came along in my life to make me feel I had more to give, that I had special qualities. She made me feel good about myself."

Out On Our Own

After high school and the divorce of his parents, Brian moved out of the basement and rented a small apartment. As a youngster, he earned money mowing lawns, and when he turned 16, he became a busboy and dishwasher. Later, he was employed at the Standard Oil service station at 51st Street and Villard, where he learned to perform oil changes, tire rotations, and tune-ups. He worked at a cabinet shop, delivered auto parts, and was employed by a trucking company. "They were all good experiences," Brian recalls. "There was not a terrible job among them."

In the 1970s, the Milwaukee Briggs & Stratton plant turned out aluminum four-cycle gasoline engines for lawn mowers, generators, and pumps at the rate of two million a year.

These were good, well-paying jobs, and Brian wanted a chance to work there. The aunt who had reared his mother was a long-time employee and put in a good word for her hard-working nephew. "I got in," Brian says. "I started out as a laborer and worked there for fifteen years.

It was good pay, so we could get an apartment and then get a house. I don't think we had lofty goals at that time."

As Brian worked at Briggs & Stratton, Linda searched for another job. Linda recalls, "I heard there was a position open at Evinrude Motors. I started as a clerk/typist for the sales manager, Bob Rudolph. "He was a fabulous boss," Linda remembers. "Even if you did something wrong, you always left his office feeling good about yourself. He was just an excellent person. He never made you feel inadequate. He always made you feel you were valued, even if you messed up."

On occasion, Linda took dictation for the chairman of the board and, at times, met with the company's legendary founder, Ralph Evinrude. "He had to be close to seventy," Linda says. "Every time we saw the man, he had the same briefcase, the same pair of shoes, and the same well-worn brown overcoat. You would never suspect he was a multi-millionaire."

Linda started her Evinrude career as a clerk/typist I. She steadily moved up the ladder: clerk/typist II, then secretary I, secretary II, and finally, senior secretary I and II. That was as far as a woman could progress at Evinrude. "I was promoted to senior secretary, which is the furthest any woman ever went in that company. There were no women at that time in any type of managerial positions."

Good Money, A New Boss, What Could Be Better?

Linda was twenty years old. "I was making good money, back then," she says. "I was making about $15,000 a year, and for someone who didn't go to college, my parents thought I hit the jackpot. Then I was promoted to work for the credit manager as his personal secretary."

Linda's new boss towered over those around him, and he had few friends within the company. "None of the other executives ever went out to lunch with him," Linda describes her new boss. "He was kind of a loner. Just not friendly."

In addition to serving as a personal secretary, Linda was responsible for collecting overdue accounts from various government agencies that purchased Evinrude products, such as the U.S. Army. "I had the government accounts, and I had to collect for the outboard motors," Linda explains. "Some of the government accounts were among the slowest in paying. It was challenging to get money out of them. So I called military bases all over the world, literally trying to get money. I really did a darn good job. I got them to pay their bills where a lot of people were not as successful, but my boss never, ever praised me for anything.

"We sat at cubicles, and one time I made an error. First thing in the morning, in front of everyone, the Credit Department, the Budget Department, the Advertising Department, he yelled at me. I was totally embarrassed. I was in tears, in the bathroom, and the girls felt so bad for me. I'll never forget.

"He had this ugly, pea soup green coffee cup with a brown pipe on it. I was expected to clean his coffee cup every morning, scrub out the dried-on coffee grinds. There I was, in the bathroom, sobbing, washing that coffee cup, and the grounds always would get hard at the bottom. I saw the toilet bowl and I took the cup and dipped it in the bowl. Now, there wasn't anything in the bowl, so I could have done worse. All the girls laughed. We were in hysterics. And then I took a napkin, and just let the cup drip-dry. I filled his cup with coffee and placed it on his desk, and all of us were just waiting for him to take his first sip. It was hysterical. That's probably one of the worst things I've ever done in my life, but I still think, well, it was well-deserved."

At Evinrude, Linda learned a valuable lesson about people and managing others. "Mr. Rudolph was loved by everybody, and he had a presence. Even when you did something wrong, you still wanted to please him, to do better for him. With the other boss, it was like you didn't care. You just started to dislike the man. You didn't want to do your best for him.

"I was so miserable working for him that I started thinking about doing something else."

Brian & Linda

3: READY, SET, LET'S GET GOING

Newlyweds Linda and Brian celebrate their nuptials at Lei Lani Hawaiian-Polynesian restaurant in Waukesha, Wisconsin.

It's Raining. No, We're Being Showered With Love

On a warm August evening in 1977, Brian was in the kitchen of his small apartment, cooking a special meal for Linda. "You're such a good cook, I think I'll marry you someday," she laughed, stealing a taste from the scrumptious concoction simmering on the stovetop.

"Why not?" Brian shot back.

"Why not what?" Linda reacted.

Brian reasoned: "We love each other, don't we? So, why not get married?"

Over dinner, Linda's lighthearted comment about getting married became the basis for a serious conversation and by evening's end, the young couple decided that, yes, the time was right. They consulted their families and set the date: Saturday, December 17.

"There was a lot to do in only four months to plan a wedding," Linda says. "My mother and father helped and so did Brian's family."

Peace Lutheran Church at 51st and Hampton was selected. The big Saturday arrived overcast and raining, but Linda remembers, "The church was beautiful, decorated for Christmas with poinsettias," and the candles burned warm and bright for the 4:00 p.m. nuptials.

"Since it was raining, we said we were being showered with love," Linda says. More than two hundred friends and family filled the church. There were schoolmates from John Marshall, co-workers from Evinrude and from Briggs & Stratton, members of the German club from Linda's youth, uncles and aunts from Brian's extended family, and many other well-wishers.

Following the ceremony, the wedding party drove the twenty-three miles to Waukesha and what was then a Wisconsin landmark, the Lei Lani Hawaiian-Polynesian Restaurant. Under palm trees and thatch, Linda, Brian, family, and friends celebrated.

Brian's uncle, Leo Kuchenreuther, operated a flourishing roofing business in South Florida and, with Aunt Sue, made his home in Ft. Lauderdale. "After the wedding, come on down to Lauderdale," Uncle Leo offered the newlyweds. "You can stay at our place, and we'll even loan you the car so you can take in the sights."

On the Monday following the wedding, Linda and Brian flew to Ft. Lauderdale. Uncle Leo and Aunt Sue met them at the airport and surprised them with a wedding night in one of the city's top hotels. In the week to come, Linda and Brian enjoyed the restaurants and attractions of Miami and South Florida. True to his word, Uncle Leo gave them the keys to his Cadillac, so they could cruise South Beach in style.

Why Is Your Back So Red?

It was on their vacation in Florida that Brian and Linda learned about the healing powers of aloe vera. Lying on the beach to get a rich, brown tan, Brian instead got a blistering, red burn. Uncle Leo took one look at Brian's back and headed to the backyard, returning with a few leaves from an aloe vera plant. "My uncle broke the leaves and drizzled the pure aloe over the burn," Brian recalls. "It really helped, and the blisters and redness disappeared. All with little bits and pieces of aloe."

Racing To The Money Pit

In the summer, the newlyweds spent weekends at Uncle Eddie Kay's cabin on Lake Nemahbin, a popular retreat twenty-seven miles west of Milwaukee. Moonlight on the lake, long walks under a towering canopy of old-growth oaks and walnuts, and just getting away for a few days made for very special memories. The peacefulness of swimming in a crystal clear Wisconsin lake was only a brief respite from the roar of drag racing. When not working, Brian was racing. Linda was at his side.

"Every weekend for many years, we raced our cars at Great Lakes Dragway in Union Grove, Wisconsin. We drove the car out there, changed the tires, removed the exhaust, and raced," Brian says, a lift in his voice. "We won trophies and when we could afford a better car to race, we towed it behind our regular car to the dragway. Linda pretty much complained the whole time."

Linda defends her racing objections. "Racing became a money pit. Something would break on the car, and everything would cost hundreds, if not thousands of dollars. And you see this kind of money going into something that has no lasting value.

"I'm thinking, what is this going to bring us for the

future? As a young couple starting out, I was the ambitious one that got tired of working for somebody else," Linda says. "I was the one looking for other possibilities. It was, my gosh, the month isn't over, but the money is gone."

Linda was restless. She remembers those early days of married life, "Everything we had, including our furniture, was hand-me-down. I started to think differently. I decided I wanted something more in my life. I think once you get through that rebellious stage, and you finally find your partner, you start to look at life a little differently. I wanted to accomplish something. I had a mate. I had a best friend. I wanted to do something worthwhile, and I didn't want to be a secretary forever. I knew that our skills were limited, because we didn't have a college education. I knew that I could always get a job as a secretary.

"I was fortunate to meet someone that became my first mentor, and she started getting me to think differently about things. I met some really good people that were able to awaken something in me that wasn't there before."

Meet Ruth Borum, Direct Seller

"I was having some skin challenges, and a friend told me about a woman she knew who had these skin-care products that were supposed to be really good," Linda relates. "I didn't know anything about direct selling, but I called her and started using the products. My skin improved."

The direct seller, Ruth Borum, representing Viviane Woodard, was about to change Linda and Brian's lives for the better. Ruth operated a Viviane Woodard boutique and demonstrated the products at home parties. In the 1970s, the Viviane Woodard name rivaled Mary Kay in popularity. The make-up base, originally developed for Olympic-swimmer-turned-film-star, Esther Williams, was part of a then-revolutionary concept in skin care, a three-part program of cleansing, toning, and moisturizing.

"Prior to this, a woman might use a jar of Pond's Cold Cream. Viviane Woodard was among the first to offer three products that worked together as a system," Linda says. "I started using this system and the products. Ruth and I became friends. I told her about my job, how I hated it and that I was looking for another secretarial position. She started talking to me about direct selling. Well, when I heard the word 'selling,' I thought, 'Oh my, I can't sell. I've never sold anything.' She just said to me, 'Think about it, and why don't you come to one of our meetings?'"

Soon after, Brian accompanied Linda to their first Viviane Woodard meeting. Linda listened as Viviane Woodard Beauty Advisors talked about their direct selling businesses. "I remember at the meeting," Linda says, "I was thinking, 'I use these products. I like them. If I join, I could buy them at a discount.' That was really the attitude I had. But I really liked this woman. I really liked her."

Linda purchased the new beauty consultant starter kit containing products and sales aids. "I didn't do much with it right away, except buy my products at wholesale," she says. "Then things at my job just got steadily worse. I started disliking it more and more."

By then, the young couple had purchased their first home, a modest three-bedroom on West Mill Road in the northwest suburbs. The monthly mortgage: about $500.

"I needed the Evinrude job so we could make the mortgage payments," Linda recalls, "But I was complaining all weekend about going back to work. And actually, I was becoming physically ill. I took a leave of absence for one week, and told everyone I had the flu. When I went back to work, I began to get these horrible pounding headaches."

She demonstrated the Viviane Woodard products at a few home parties. Her hosts were some of the women she worked with at Evinrude. One evening, Linda returned home after a Viviane Woodard party. She was beaming. "I sold over one hundred dollars tonight!" she excitedly told her husband.

Go Do More Of That

Brian was astonished. "I'm thinking, 'People spend one hundred dollars on that stuff? Holy cow.' I was really impressed, and I did a lot of encouraging. 'Go do more of that. What can I do, so you can do that more?'"

Even with Brian's encouragement, Linda faced self-doubt. "It was scary," she says. "It was a big, scary deal for me, because sales was something that never in a million years had entered my mind. Deep down, I was a very shy person. You know, being tall – when you grow up being tall like I was – and I never really dated. I didn't blossom until about ninth grade. The other girls back in junior high went to dances, and boys would ask them. Well, no one ever asked me, because I was so much taller than the boys. I felt like the ugly duckling. All my girlfriends would have boyfriends over, they got little love notes, and none of that happened for me, until I turned fifteen. Then I started to learn how to wear a little makeup, and I really developed my own style.

"So it was a real scary deal for me, talking to people, and the confidence wasn't quite there, yet. I had good people skills. People always liked me, because I was never a threat to anyone. I can get along with everybody. I make a sale and get excited. And I'd get this feeling of 'Wow, this is really neat.' Then people started telling me they liked the product, that it was doing something for them, and I felt I had not just made money, but I helped this person. So those two good feelings were coming together.

"Meanwhile things at work were getting more miserable. One day, I went around to my coworkers, most of these women were in their 40s, some in their 50s. They had been at Evinrude forever. They had the gold anniversary watch or their little pin for their years of service. I asked them, 'Are you glad you stayed with Evinrude?' Back then, Evinrude was a very secure place to be."

Linda "interviewed" as many as eight veteran Evinrude secretaries. This is what they told her:

"Oh, if I could do it all over again..."

"If I was young again..."

"I should have done this..." or "I could have done that..."

"If I could start all over, I would have done something different with my life."

Astounded by the outpouring of unfulfilled careers, Linda concluded, "I don't want to sound like this when I'm 40 years old. I don't want to have to be in a place where no one is truly happy, where you work to just get by."

Quit And Don't Come Home Until You Do

Linda realized she wanted more. At Evinrude, she says, "We watched that clock – the bell rang at noon for lunchtime, and the bell rang at 4:30. And that's what we lived for, the breaks and the bells. And I'm thinking, 'I don't want to ever end up like this.' It was Labor Day weekend, and again I was moaning and groaning about having to go to work on Tuesday."

Brian stopped her in mid-groan. "You know what? I've really had it. When you go back to work on Tuesday, give your notice and don't come home until you do."

On the one hand, Linda reasoned, her Viviane Woodard business was beginning to pay some of the household bills. "I was getting repeat business, and I liked the fact there was money coming in while I was at my day job. I wasn't even doing anything, and people were placing orders." On the other hand, to leave a secure job and steady paycheck was downright frightening.

She thought, "You know, Evinrude isn't really all that bad."

Brian offered this advice: "What's the worst that can happen? If you're not successful with Viviane Woodard fulltime, you can always be a secretary."

"Brian was right," Linda says. "I could always find a secretarial job, and I liked my Viviane Woodard business. Going to opportunity meetings, training classes, and when I left these meetings, I felt so much better, with more self-esteem, a more positive outlook. I liked the idea of helping other women by offering these great products."

Adds Brian, "We saw other people earning at least a livable income. We knew this business was a real deal."

"Our direct selling business was starting to become a way of life," says Linda. "My thinking started to change. Things that I thought at one time would be impossible were now looking like, well, why couldn't it be possible?"

But quit a good job? "I was afraid of quitting the job because you're programmed that way," Linda continues. "You're brought up to go to school, get an education, get a job. You get married, you buy a little house, have a couple of kids, pay off your house, and you're done in life. That's how I was – that was my family's definition of success at the time. I wasn't encouraged to think big."

On the Tuesday following Labor Day, heart pounding in her chest, Linda watched the clock on the wall tick through the minutes of the day. It was now 4:25 p.m. It was now or never. "It took all day to get up my courage, and I was very nervous, because we had this mortgage now," Linda recalls of that fateful day. "I went into my boss's office, and said I was giving my two weeks' notice. When I told him what I was going to do, he laughed at me.

"He was a big, booming man, you know, big guy in every sense of the word, big ears, big head. He looked at me and said, 'You're never going to make it. You're just a little fish in the sea.'

"He said, 'You'll be eaten up by, you know, what's that company? Mary Kay? You're never going to make it. All those big cosmetic companies, and you're going to try to make a living selling lipstick?' That's what he said to me. I left his office feeling so very small. I cried all the way home. I'm thinking, he's right, I'm not going to make it. What did I just do?"

Linda achieves "Queen of Sales."

4: THE BUSINESS WITHIN A BUSINESS

Need Cash? Work More Hours

Without Linda's income, it was suddenly more difficult to make ends met. "We ate Campbell's Soup and
white bread," Brian remembers what happened next. "We
had the mortgage and the other bills. We had faith the
Viviane Woodard business would eventually pay more, but
in direct sales, the money doesn't start rolling in, even if
you start working full time."

Says Linda, "There was enough good happening in
the business, and somehow we were able to see the bigger
picture."

Until the Viviane Woodard career took off, Brian
searched for a second job and found it at a hydraulics factory located near the Milwaukee Airport. Problem was, the
new job was during the day, the same hours he was employed at Briggs & Stratton. Talking with his supervisors
at Briggs & Stratton, Brian worked out a plan. He would
report to work at the hydraulics plant at 7:00 a.m. and work
the first shift until 2:00 p.m., hop in his car, and drive from
the south side of Milwaukee to Briggs & Stratton on the
north side in time to report at 3:00 p.m. for the second shift.
His workday would end at 11:00 p.m. He would need to be
up early the next morning to make the drive to the hydraulics plant to start all over again. This grueling routine continued for more than a year.

"The income from Linda selling cosmetics and my
second job came close to equaling the pay Linda previously
earned at Evinrude," Brian says. Despite the long hours,
there was an important benefit. Linda was happier. The
headaches stopped, and so did the weekend complaining.

I'll Clean, You Sell

In the months to come, the Viviane Woodard checks
grew in size, and eventually Brian gave up the hydraulics

factory job. To free Linda's time to develop her Viviane Woodard business, Brian assumed the household chores, including the cooking, laundry, and cleaning. To this day, he handles most of the cooking in the Kaminski household. "As for cleaning the house," he says with a broad smile, "I eventually decided to hire someone to do that part."

Taking on responsibilities to free up Linda so she had more time to sell and sponsor new Beauty Advisors became Brian's modus operandi. "I did whatever I could," he explains. "I could do the bookwork. I could handle the inventory. I could do the banking. I could do everything required of the business with the exception of selling the cosmetics and offering the business opportunity. That's what Linda did best."

Years later, at L'Bri, Brian adheres to the same philosophy. The home office ships the product to the customer, mails the catalogs, follows up with emails and postcards, takes care of much of the day-to-day business so L'Bri Consultants have more time to meet with customers and sell.

You're An Outstanding Achiever

Linda's Viviane Woodard business was growing. They remodeled the third bedroom into an office. At the end of that first year working fulltime with Viviane Woodard products, Linda Kaminski was doing so well, Ruth Borum invited her to the company's national convention. The year was 1981.

Along with Ruth and her husband, Vance, Linda and Brian flew to Las Vegas for the annual Viviane Woodard Beauty Advisors Convention. It was a grand affair at the luxurious Riviera Hotel. More than five hundred Beauty Advisors from throughout the nation participated in general sessions featuring business-oriented workshops and parties. "In a skit, we were Mr. and Mrs. Success, and we had a rainbow and a pot of gold," Linda recalls. "Brian wore a big ten-gallon hat, and I borrowed an old fur coat from his grandmother's attic."

Linda earns the "Outstanding Newcomer of the Year" award at the 1981 Viviane Woodard National Convention in Las Vegas

In the ballroom of the Riviera Hotel, Linda's mentor, Ruth Borum, left, displays her "Queen of Sales" award. At right is Linda, the Viviane Woodard "Outstanding Newcomer of the Year."

The highlight of the convention was the gala awards banquet. Linda purchased a lovely gown to wear. "It cost more than I wanted to spend, because it had cutwork and beading, but I thought, 'Well, I'll just have to sell a little more product to pay for it.'"

The Borums, Kaminskis, and two other couples shared one of the more than sixty gaily-dressed tables in the hotel's exquisite ballroom. Company executives announced the names of Viviane Woodard's top achievers. Then it happened. The audience heard: "This year, we are proud that our Outstanding Newcomer of the Year is Linda Kaminski, here from Milwaukee, Wisconsin."

"I was shocked," Linda remembers that emotional moment. "You know, you can't believe you heard that right. No. It can't be. Then you're looking at the people next to you, as if to ask, 'Did you hear what I heard?' Your heart's pounding a million miles an hour, and the butterflies are in your stomach. You're nervous. You're wondering, what's happening here, because it's never happened before.

"To walk up – the lights – the music playing. You're walking up to a stage with a podium. Next to the podium you've got these big tables with all the awards, and there's the president of the company, the CEO, all these important people, and there you are. I was totally awe-struck."

Accepting the "Outstanding Newcomer of the Year" Award, Linda was asked to say a few words. "I don't remember what came out of my mouth," she admits. "In my entire life, I had never received an award. All I remember is that when I returned to our table, Vance said, 'Congratulations. In the future, we're going to have to work on your acceptance speeches.'"

That same night, Ruth Borum, Linda's sponsor and friend, was named the company's sales leader for the year and presented the "Queen of Sales" sash, like those worn by Miss America.

By the end of the weekend convention, wearing her

own "Newcomer" sash, Linda remembers "feeling like a princess." Linda says, "We had been whisked away to another world, the glamour, the success stories, and just meeting other women who told their stories and to hear how they overcame challenges in their lives and in their businesses. I could relate to them. Experiencing all this, my emotions got all crazy inside. I remember realizing, 'Wow, there's so much more for me out there.'

"That was my first convention, and it was wonderful. It was really life-changing. Everything changes when you come back from a convention like that."

Linda, second from left, achieves "Queen of Sales" honors at Viviane Woodard

Star Performer "Queen Of Sales"

Linda fondly credits Ruth Borum as "my very first mentor in life. She really got me to understand the benefits of the direct selling industry and believing in myself. She literally groomed me from head to toe and told me how to dress. I had those cloggy platform shoes and wore a suit with them. Ruth would say, 'Those shoes don't go with that outfit.' She helped me so much, and she always did it in a way that was encouraging and supportive."

Brian agrees. "Vance and Ruth were a husband-wife team, and we were a husband-wife team. We learned a lot from them. They really guided us. They were very good business people and very good friends."

In the years to follow, Linda, with Brian in his supporting role, continued to be a Viviane Woodard star performer. Following in the footsteps of her mentor, Linda was "Queen of Sales" four times.

Where Burns Are Just Part Of The Job

For workers in the Briggs & Stratton foundry, burns came with the territory. Molten aluminum in excess of 1,220 degrees Fahrenheit was poured into dies for casting the block and parts of lawnmower engines. "In the years I was with Briggs & Stratton, I worked in the aluminum foundry, in die casting, which is always very hot and dirty. I had a couple of really big burns, and many small burns on my arms and chest, but so did everyone else," Brian says about working on the shop floor. "It was just part of the job."

On this particular day in 1985, at about noon, Brian was driving a stand-up forklift. "These were backwards forklifts," he describes the motorized trucks. "You stood in a way that the forklift was actually behind you. When you drove, you went backwards, so there was nothing in front of you. I was driving my forklift down an aisle.

"Another employee, also using a forklift, was delivering the molten metal. On the front of his forklift was a great big pot containing the molten metal. There was a lid on the pot and two spouts, one on each side. He drove his forklift to the die cast machines, poured the liquid aluminum into these little holding tanks where the metal was scooped out and formed into parts.

"I was driving one way, and the other guy was driving towards me with his pot full of molten metal. Neither one of us saw the other. Suddenly, he saw me, slammed on the brakes, and the metal kept coming."

Like a wave splashing over a break wall, super-heated aluminum spewed from the pot, soaking Brian Kaminski from the waist to the floor. Protected by only cotton work pants and shoes, his skin was instantly charred with third-degree burns. "I whipped my pants down to my ankles and ran down the aisle" headed for the nurse's aid station. "I was in shock, and this must have been on Thursday, because paydays were Thursday. As I ran down the aisle heading to the nurse, my boss, Irv said, 'Oh, Brian, before you go, let me give you your check; and he handed me my paycheck. I was thinking, 'This is weird,' but I took it and said, 'Okay, thanks, Irv.'"

The nurse on duty took one look at Brian's injuries and dialed Emergency 9-1-1. Still clutching the pay envelope, Brian arrived by ambulance at St. Joseph Hospital.

How Soon Can You Get Here?

The phone in the Kaminski home rang. Linda picked up the receiver. "This is St. Joseph Hospital Burn Unit. Your husband was brought in. How soon can you get here?"

Linda returned the phone to the cradle. "I really didn't understand how serious this was," Linda recalls of that frightening day. "Brian had been coming home all the time with burns. In his work, splatter burns were not something new. But I had never gotten a call like this. He was in the hospital? That must mean it's a little more of a burn than he normally has."

Linda drove to St. Joseph and made her way to the Burn Unit. "I really didn't know what to expect," she says. "When I saw him, I knew it was serious."

Brian's father arrived a few minutes later. They were shocked by the extent of the burns. "It was really gory looking," Brian remembers, and the pain was intense. A nurse gave him an injection for tetanus, antibiotics to prevent infection, and more drugs to deaden the pain. "I never had a shot in my whole life," Brian says. "I was actually getting multiple shots of medicine, so that was traumatic for me."

His upper thigh wrapped in bandages, Brian stayed the night in the Burn Unit, but was discharged the following day, because it wasn't a full-body burn.

The doctor and nurse told Linda how to treat the injury. "The skin was raw and oozing and all the things you can imagine that go along with a serious burn," she says. "So, of course, I listened very intently about what I had to do to change the dressing and put on this salve the doctor prescribed, and all the other details that go along with having a burn. We went home with the salve and painkillers."

This Is Not Working

At the pharmacy, Linda purchased boxes of gauze. "I had to change the dressing," she recalls, "but every time I changed the dressing, it was impossible to strip away the bandage without re-injuring the wound."

"It got worse and in a few days I could hardly walk," Brian describes the ordeal. "I was really bandaged up, and it wasn't healing that well."

"We kept up with this routine for four or five days, and nothing was improving," Linda says. "Brian was still in pain and oozing like crazy, and it just wasn't making sense. It seemed every time I would remove a dressing, I would make the wounds that much worse."

Confiding in Ruth Borum about the treatment, Linda told her Brian did not seem to be progressing. Ruth was emphatic. "She told me, 'That salve is doing nothing but suffocating his skin.' Of course, I'm thinking, 'Well, what does she know? She's not a nurse.' But still, I respected her, and she said, 'You've got to get moisture back into that, and you've got to let it breathe,' and she started telling me about aloe."

Linda and Brian knew about aloe for minor burns, remembering how Uncle Leo treated Brian's back on their wedding trip. Convinced of the healing nature of aloe, the couple sold an aloe vera gel product to their customers to treat insect bites, scrapes, and burns. But use aloe on a serious wound? "This was way beyond something you'd get from a hot stove or a sunburn," Linda thought. "You're in a hospital, and they tell you what to do, but I listened to Ruth. At this point, I thought we had nothing more to lose because the salve and bandages were not working."

Linda went to the basement storeroom and took several of the four-ounce tubes of the aloe product from inventory, unwrapped the bandages, and using sterile gauze, spread aloe on the wounds. There was an immediate burning sensation, but within a few minutes the burning subsided, replaced by a soothing coolness.

"We watched and waited," Brian says.

"He had a hard time sleeping at night because he couldn't really turn, and there were no bandages. He was always pretty much in one position," Linda adds.

I Think This Aloe Is Helping

The next morning, they observed "a slight improvement." Linda says, "At first we thought, 'Are we imagining things?' But we both felt there was improvement, and he didn't seem to be in the same amount of pain.'"

That day, Linda applied layers of aloe to her husband's burns. "It was thick, goopy, and gloppy, and then it would just sit there. The oozing started to subside. The skin wasn't peeling, because we weren't using gauze, and he just started to progress and got better, and better, and better," Linda says.

On the follow-up visit to the doctor, the physician scolded them for not following his instructions. "He gave us a long lecture about how lucky we were that a major infection hadn't settled into the skin," Linda relates. "The salve had certain things in it to help ward off infection, and there was a reason to keep the wounds covered, and I listened to the doctor, and I tried to explain to him, 'Yes, but nothing was happening. He was in pain. The burns were not improving. The skin was sore. It was hot. Then we do this aloe treatment, and we see results. We did not have infections, because we didn't live in an unclean environment."

The doctor insisted they drop the aloe and return to the salve and bandages. "We left there thinking, we're not going to do it, and we didn't," explains Linda.

Linda and Brian were convinced aloe contained miraculous properties. "The experience with Brian's burns was our first big WOW," Linda continues. "His skin kept healing. I thought for sure he was going to have scarring, because there were actual holes in his skin. When you get a burn like that, there are ugly holes and you think, 'How can that tissue ever grow back?" But it did. We used tubes of that product, tubes of it. I think we used up a couple of tubes every single day, because we just plastered it on. Today, you would never even know he had burns on his thigh."

"We just felt good about the aloe," Brian says. "So we kept using it, and I kept getting better. There was no scarring. It was just incredible, and the doctors and nurses were all amazed how well my burn healed. We attributed it to the aloe, and because of this, we love aloe vera."

Brian was off work a period of four weeks recovering from the accident. This was by far the most serious burn he experienced at his job, but it wasn't the last. About a year later, he opened the radiator cap on a hot forklift. Boiling water sprayed his chest. Brian treated the burn with the same aloe product and was completely healed.

Linda and Brian check into the Sheraton Waikiki for a five-night vacation, earned as a top Viviane Woodard achiever. This is the first of two incentive trips to Hawaii.

You Mean, We Can Go To Hawaii?

Looking through the stacks of letters, magazines, and free offers that arrived in the mail that day in 1987, Linda pulled out a colorful circular. It was from Viviane Woodard, announcing a new incentive contest. The top prize: an all-expenses paid vacation in Hawaii. In a previous Viviane Woodard contest, she earned a trip to Catalina Island. But Hawaii! Determined to take her husband, Linda set monthly goals, worked the hours, held extra "lessons" to demonstrate the products, and by year's end, earned the trip – for two! The Kaminskis left the mainland for the first time, jetting west to Honolulu.

Along with thirty other couples, all Viviane Woodard achievers, they checked into the Sheraton Waikiki for a five-night vacation of a lifetime, including luxury hotel, gourmet meals, soaking up the rays on the beach, and touring the Fiftieth State's attractions. "One evening, we had a meal where every person on the trip had a personal waiter," Linda says. "Dressed in white, with the white gloves, holding your silver tray, in unison they lifted the covers off and presented this amazing meal. It was clockwork – boom, boom, boom, and it was beautiful."

They took in the Don Ho Show. "Back then, he was a real star," Brian laughs. "We were treated so very special, like we had never been treated before. The meals were incredible. The hotel was beautiful with the palm trees and the pool area. We were living a dream."

Continues Brian, "It was very motivating. We wanted more of this. This was the lifestyle for us."

A top Viviane Woodard achiever in sales and sponsoring, Linda earns a vacation to the Queen Mary Hotel, Long Beach, California.

Adds Linda, "We just loved it and won every trip

thereafter with the company." These adventures included trips to the Queen Mary in California, a spa experience in Arizona, and a second trip to Hawaii, this time to the Big Island. Regardless of destination, Linda most enjoyed "the camaraderie" with other Beauty Advisors, "the bonding, getting to know one another, and sharing future dreams and goals. It was like an extended family.

"Every night, we returned to our room and had something waiting for us, a little gift, perhaps a special picture frame or a Waterford crystal letter opener engraved with the Viviane Woodard logo and the year of the trip. So every aspect of the trip was great. And the fact that here was an extra treat for just doing your job. At the same time we were earning this trip, we were increasing our business and our income."

When Viviane Woodard introduces an automobile sales incentive program in 1987, Linda is among the first Beauty Advisors to earn a new car

In 1987, Viviane Woodard introduced a new sales incentive. The reward: the lease on a new car. Linda soon qualified, and the Kaminskis picked up the car at a Milwaukee dealership.

Brian gave up his second job at the hydraulics factory and was earning a newfound respect from his friends and fellow employees at Briggs & Stratton. "They're saying, 'Whoa, Linda and Brian are going to Hawaii with all

Linda and Brian on their second Hawaiian vacation.

expenses paid,' like we're movie stars. The boss's boss didn't go to Hawaii. We're driving a new car, because they gave us a car," Brian says. "We're just living a dream, making good money, new car, free travel, more spending money."

What Happened To Our American Dream?

The American dream was about to become a night-mare. The first hints of trouble in paradise came as a plethora of backorders and late commission checks from the company. Then on a Friday afternoon, two weeks before Christmas, Linda went to get into her car, and it was not where she left it. "I called the police and reported the car stolen," she says. "Since it was late in the day, the Viviane Woodard offices were closed, so I waited until Monday morning to call them and report the theft." On

Monday morning, Linda called the company and learned the car was not stolen. It had been repossessed, because Viviane Woodard stopped making the lease payments.

"We were so trusting, we believed the stories the Viviane Woodard company told us," Brian says, shaking his head incredulously.

Linda agrees, "We just kept believing the company, and finally we heard that the reason we had backorders was because they weren't paying the suppliers. It became a standing joke: A customer called to place an order. She rattled off her order to us, and then said in the next breath, 'So, what don't you have?' And that was how we kept going until finally, it got to the point where I couldn't recruit anymore. I could no longer sell the benefits of the company."

Brian explains what happened: "As a company, they had some challenges. They were bought and sold a few times. There was mismanagement and embezzlement at the highest levels. We learned later that one company official was literally socking money away in a Swiss bank account." The Kaminskis, now in their early 30s, were with Viviane Woodard for eight years and were among the company's top distributors.

"We started searching for a new home," Linda says. "I was trying to find a product, first, that I could believe in. Then I called a cosmetic company I heard was doing great things. It was Finelle. They asked us questions and when they heard what kind of business we were doing, they offered to fly us out to their offices near Boston."

"We wanted samples of the products to try, and they declined to give us samples," Brian says. "They said, 'No, we'll fly you out here and give you the samples in person.'"

"They wanted to meet us," explains Linda. "So they extended this invitation, and we accepted." The Kaminskis flew to Boston, rented a car, and drove the thirty miles north to Lawrence, Massachusetts and the Finelle Cosmetics home office.

Deciding to cut ties with Viviane Woodard was "horribly stressful," and worse than any divorce one could imagine, Linda says, but after much thought, in 1989 she and Brian decided to jump ship. It had been a long-term relationship with Viviane Woodard, a company she loved with a passion. Most of Linda's downline, numbering hundreds of independent Beauty Advisors, followed her to Finelle.

Linda and Brian tour the Finelle Cosmetics home office in 1989.

Finding Success In A New Home

Similar to Viviane Woodard, Finelle skin care products were water-based, rather than the oil-base found in products then sold in many department stores. So quality was not an issue. Linda retained most of her loyal customers who then became Finelle customers.

With hard work and commitment to their direct sales business, Linda and Brian accomplished the changeover to the new company, and as Linda says, "We got things rolling again." Not quite a year with the company, Linda was celebrated for joining Finelle's "Top 10 in Sales."

"No one knew I even existed," she says. "I remember that one of the top achievers came up to me after the announcement and said, 'Where did you come from?' That was exactly what she said to me, and I was taken aback. That was how I met her. Her name was Faye, and she had earned top honors for many years, and here's this newcomer coming in at Number 10, and I hadn't even been with the company a year."

Linda earned the first Finelle trip to Cancun and invited Brian's mother to join her for a week at this Mexican resort. Next, she earned an Oldsmobile Cutlass, soon followed by a Lincoln Continental. The next year, they traveled to Montreal as part of a Finelle incentive trip, and Linda was Number 2 in the company in sales and sponsoring. In 1991, Linda achieved her goal: to be "Queen of Sales," the top distributor in the company based on sales volume and sponsoring. Her personal sales that year: $132,000.

"Finelle had Dottie's Sweetheart Club," explains Linda. "When you earned membership in Dottie's Sweetheart Club for the first time, you received a heart-shaped,

Linda in Morocco on a Finelle incentive vacation.

14-carat gold pin. For every six months that you sponsored at least eighteen people, you got a diamond for your pin. In all the years I was with Finelle, I only missed her club one time. We sponsored more people with Finelle than we did in Viviane Woodard.

"We   earned

more trips. Morocco, Venezuela, and then a second Lincoln.

"This company allowed you to keep your car, by the way. You would get a new one every four years, so we sold the first Lincoln for about $10,000, and I moved into the second Lincoln. That was a nice benefit. It was great."

Time To Get Out Of The House

"During all these years, I'm working at Briggs in the aluminum foundry," Brian says, "and helping Linda with the business. I'm ordering the inventory. I'm doing the shipping to the customers. I'm doing the bookwork, the banking, taking care of some of the repeat business, answering simple questions about skin care. I just keep learning and doing more and more, because I want Linda to have the time to focus on selling and sponsoring.

"I had a great boss at Briggs and was in the union. It was a good job." Brian pauses. "I didn't love it. I mean, I always dreamed of someday getting out of there."

When the Finelle business outgrew their home, the Kaminskis rented a small office on the second floor of a storefront building located two blocks from the Briggs & Stratton plant. Containing a thousand square feet, the office provided much-needed space for inventory and shipping. There was a spacious room for training new distributors or to conduct weekly meetings. Three small offices and a storage room rounded out the facility. "In one office, we maintained a little store, because we had customers who came to us for their Finelle products," Brian explains.

In the morning, before reporting to Briggs, Brian was in the habit of first driving to the office. "I arrived there at 5:00 a.m., did a few things for an hour and a half or so, and then went to Briggs," Brian says. "After work, I stopped back at the office, did this and that, and then came home."

During the day, Linda worked at the office. Soon they hired an office assistant.

*Linda with Andy...
Earlier that year,
Linda earned
"Queen of Sales"
honors at Finelle.*

The Queen Of Sales Delivers

It was time to start a family. "Here we are, 34 years old and married fourteen years," Brian recalls. "We're having fun going on trips and living the American Dream of direct selling, enjoying all the benefits that go along with that. Yet, there was something missing in our lives. Should we start a family? A couple of months later, Linda was pregnant."

In early August 1991, Linda was about to give birth and knew she could not attend the annual Finelle National Convention, scheduled that upcoming weekend. The company's president, accompanied by a photographer, flew to Milwaukee to present the "Queen of Sales" award. The official photo of the presentation was shown at the convention's banquet and later printed in the Finelle magazine for distributors. A few days later, on August 9, Linda gave birth to their son, Andrew.

"We kind of spoiled their convention, because their Queen of Sales was not there," Brian says sheepishly.

Despite taking time off to care for their baby, the family's Finelle income grew thirty percent that year. Linda credits the nature of direct selling, the ability of independent sales Consultants to "duplicate" themselves. "In direct selling, the independent sales person sponsors others into the business, teaching them what she knows about selling and sponsoring," she explains. "It is said she is duplicating herself." Since the members of the team continue selling, the direct seller can take a break from the business and still earn income. Marvels Linda, "In direct sales, if you take care of your business, your business will take care of you. My customers and sales team were very loyal to me, and our business continued to grow and prosper."

With Linda leading Finelle in sales and sponsoring,
she and Brian live the American Dream.

Quit Your Job. Are You Guys Crazy?

Every so often, Brian vowed to his foundry co-workers that someday he would quit his job and help Linda with the direct selling business fulltime. "Right, you're going to sell lipstick," they would say and then laugh uproariously. "You'll never quit," they assured him.

"They teased me quite a bit about our business, but I pretty much let it roll off me, because I really believed I would quit someday," Brian says. "Then one day, our bonus checks from Finelle were enough that we didn't really need my income from Briggs anymore. I wanted to stay home to help with Andy. It made sense to quit, so I met with my boss and turned in my notice."

Brian's father was understandably skeptical: "First Linda quits her job, and now you quit your job. Are you guys crazy?"

That year, Linda led the company in sales and sponsoring. Their sales organization was Finelle's largest. "We were earning over $100,000 a year and living the American Dream," Brian says. "Cars, vacations, everything we needed. It was great."

Have You Heard? Your Office Is On Fire!

One evening at a Milwaukee hotel, Linda was speaking to a group of new distributors, teaching them about the business and the benefits of selling Finelle products. Brian was near the meeting room's door when one of their Beauty Advisors approached him. "Have you heard?" she blurted out excitedly. "Your office is on fire."

Dumbfounded, Brian stared at her. "What are you talking about?"

The distributor repeated her statement, this time flailing her arms for emphasis. "Your office is on fire. Your office is on fire." They found a television in the hotel bar and turned the channel to the breaking news. "Sure enough," Brian says. "There was our office, up in flames and burning down." Linda was upset and so were her many distributors as they gathered around the TV newscast. Brian took a deep breath. "Well, okay, just take it easy everyone. It's just a building, and no one is hurt."

Brian called the landlord and then, with Linda at his side, drove to the location of their office. The fire department was still putting out the flames, but it was obviously a total loss. Inventory, tax records, some cash, and many personal items in storage there, including irreplaceable family photographs, were destroyed in the blaze. It was later determined the fire started on the structure's first floor in a roasted chicken carryout restaurant.

The day after the fire, Linda searches the wreckage of their former office.

The next morning, in daylight, Linda and Brian inspected the remains of their business. There was not much to see. "We were pretty devastated," Brian says. "It was a total loss, and we were underinsured. We lost maybe $20,000 worth of inventory and all the office equipment. Everything was gone."

Not quite everything. Digging through the ashes,

they came upon the Swingline stapler and, in another corner, the fax machine.

Returning home, they took stock. One stapler, without staples. One fax machine, covered in soot. That was it. If they turned the house into an office, they reasoned, they could continue the business. Two bedrooms became offices. The basement was the warehouse. To get them back on their feet, Finelle immediately shipped $5,000 in merchandise. "They said, 'Here you go,'" Brian remembers. "'You don't have to pay us back.' Finelle was very nice and very generous."

Please, Shop Out Of Our Van

In the months and years before the fire, Linda operated a boutique-style shop at the office on Saturdays. Customers came to the shop between 10:00 a.m. and 2:00 p.m. to purchase skin care and beauty products. "Saturday was a big selling day for us," Linda says. "We typically sold as much as $2,000 on a Saturday."

Fearing her long-time customers would be coming to the office and finding a burned-out hulk, Linda improvised. She called and sent faxes to some of her customers, informing them about the fire, but knew there were many more customers she could not reach as easily. The shipment from Finelle arrived. "We had a black van at that time," Linda says. "I put everything in our van and drove to the parking lot of the former office. I had a little box with my change in it. People came. I told them about the fire and sold out of the back of the van."

At 2:00 p.m., Linda counted her sales. Surprisingly, they totaled just over one thousand dollars.

In the following weeks, Linda phased out the boutique on wheels, opting to accept orders by phone and fax, and ship by UPS. "But it just shows," Linda says, "you can make anything work, if you really just think about it.

That's something Brian and I are both really good at," she continues. "We can be in the pits, but we don't stay there long. We figure something out. What can I create here? What can we do? There's a way to turn this thing around. We're learning something from this, and it's going to be a good experience. Generally, when we hit adversity, we turn it around and make it work."

Coming back after the fire was a challenge for both Brian and Linda, yet they persevered. "We got everything rolling again, except for the smell," Brian says. "There's something about the smell of things that just never goes away."

"We really believed in the direct selling industry," Brian says, and Finelle was a great company. "Everything was wonderful," Linda remembers. Their income was higher than ever before. They earned trips to exotic locations. A new Lincoln Continental, paid for by Finelle, was parked in their driveway.

Trouble In Paradise, A Second Time Around

According to Brian, Finelle was started by Dottie Feigenbaum and her husband, Maury. "She passed away, unfortunately, and then the company was managed by Maury and his son," Brian says.

The next incentive trip was to Barbados and true to form, Linda earned the vacation for herself and Brian. Invited to a special dinner, the company's top producers were handed a bitter pill. The president of the company announced Finelle was changing the compensation plan. Linda's income would drop thirty percent immediately.

The bombshell and the condescending way the company president addressed these high achieving women upset Linda. "He was from Wall Street, and he took his Wall Street personality and used it with all these women. Just the verbiage that was used, he would say to the gals at one of the dinners, 'You know, women really don't know how to run a business. What you ladies do well is you talk a lot.' This is what he said to these million dollar producers at dinner. Somebody would lose their car and then earn it back. He said, 'Well, you got your car back, that's great. Do you think you can keep it this time?' That is not what I expect someone in his position to say to his sales field. You know, you find new companies, you believe in them, and yet these things happen."

Furious and discouraged, Linda seriously considered getting out of direct sales. "I was ready to chuck it all and move to Arizona and open a submarine sandwich shop. That was really what I was thinking."

Happy Birthday, And By The Way

Says Brian, "It was happening to us, again. We were doing our thing, selling and sponsoring, training and doing everything we needed to do, and then the company did something like this that changed everything. And this happened real quick. It was unexpected. At Viviane Woodard, there were signs, such as the car being repossessed, but this one, all of a sudden, boom, one day you turned around and your monthly check was $2,500 less."

Linda was exasperated. "We had been through a transition once, going from one company to another company. This was a challenge, to rebuild your business and work to be on top again. I thought, 'Am I crazy? Maybe this isn't the right thing for me anymore.' Then we received this call, out of the blue, while in Barbados."

The call in Barbados, as it turned out, was not quite "out of the blue." Unknown to Linda, Brian had telephoned the president of Viviane Woodard to wish her a happy birthday. During the call, he mentioned the surprise compensation change.

She called back, had a brief conversation with Brian,

and Brian booked the next flight out of Barbados. His destination: Southern California.

They Want You Back

"Brian left early, and I stayed with our group on the trip," Linda says. "When I arrived home, the first thing I heard was, 'We are going out to L.A. We've been given this offer. The company's now out of bankruptcy, and everything is in order, and they want you back.'"

When Linda was associated with Viviane Woodard, she broke every sales and sponsoring record in the company's 30-year history. She was now the number one distributor at Finelle, with the highest personal and group sales, and the largest downline in the United States and Canada.

Viviane Woodard wanted her back, and they were offering an ownership deal, if she and Brian made the jump. Remembers Linda, "I was shocked, but I thought, 'Well, this will be an adventure.'"

Arriving in Los Angeles, Linda learned the company was under new management, was again solvent, and the new home office team was eager to move forward to build a stronger, better Viviane Woodard. "This was my first home, the company I grew up in, so I had a lot of love for this place," she remembers thinking. "This could be quite an opportunity to come back and do something like this."

Members of the new executive team traveled to Milwaukee to study Linda and Brian's methods. Brian explains: "They wanted to see how we processed orders, shipped to customers, followed up with customers for repeat business. Even when we were at Viviane Woodard the first time, we ran our personal business like a company inside of a company. We handled our own training. We had our own support materials. Then at Finelle, we really ran our own company within a company, because we did a lot of things differently than the company did."

Brian continues, "They brought an attorney and an independent accountant to see if everything was legit. That our business was as successful and profitable as it appeared on paper." It was.

Commute To California? Why Not?

Declining to relocate the family to California, Linda worked at home and traveled to Los Angeles for a few days each month. Under Linda and Brian's direction, Viviane Woodard revised the marketing plan to emphasize "party plan" sales, developed a new hostess program, and updated the training materials.

"For a while, it went well, but we had some challenges that were difficult to overcome," Linda relates. "In general, the company was not willing to initiate some of the changes we thought were essential for long-term growth. We were losing valuable time we needed to act quickly to re-build the sales field."

Targeting the most promising distributors, Linda traveled across the country, meeting with Beauty Advisors, stimulating sponsoring, and training the new Advisors. "I kept working with the field, developing the field and making them stronger," Linda tells of this hectic period. "On one of the trips, I went to North Carolina to work with a woman who had become stagnant. She was doing about $10,000 a month in group sales and immediately after my trip, she was up to $30,000 a month. Some things we were doing were effective and others were not so effective. It was not working as we had hoped."

After four years leading the Viviane Woodard sales field, Linda threw in the towel. She resigned as vice president of sales, and Brian turned in his notice as director of field development.

In retrospect, Brian is philosophical. "We did everything that we thought we could to help grow the company. In the end, it was a good experience. We learned a lot.

"It could have been us. I don't know what the answer was. I'm certainly not going to blame them. It had to be partly our fault, too. I mean, for whatever reason, it didn't work. We all gave it a good try."

In the basement "distribution center," L'Bri Pure n' Natural products ready for shipping. Notice the half-ounce bottles, soon to be filled with Daily Moisturizing Hand & Body Lotion.

5: A BUSINESS OF OUR OWN

Let's Go To Arizona And Open A Sub Shop

After sixteen years in direct sales, starting as a Beauty Advisor, achieving "Outstanding Newcomer" and then "Queen of Sales," developing a large and successful business, switching companies and climbing to the top all over again, working in a corporate capacity to turn a company around, it all took a toll. Linda and Brian Kaminski were physically and mentally exhausted.

Linda: "I was burned out. Disappointed. Deflated. Frustrated. It was the lowest point I can ever remember feeling. We had been through all these changes. I was tired. I thought, 'Okay, I need something totally new. I've had it with direct sales.' So I presented my idea about moving to Arizona and opening a sub shop. Brian just looked at me as if I had lost my mind."

For several minutes, Brian was silent. Neither spoke. Then he said, "You know, we're good at what we do. We just haven't had the right company behind us."

It was the sensible, practical side of Brian speaking, and Linda only half-listened, but she continued to listen. Linda remembers, "Some of what Brian was saying made sense, but I was fighting it, because I was frustrated with the people who were leading these companies and the roadblocks we continued to encounter."

Brian: "We just haven't had the right people leading us. We need to start from scratch and do it our way. We need to start our own company."

Linda's eyes widened. She was now fully engaged. "Start our own company! I couldn't even fathom everything we would need to do. We would need the product, and not any product, a great product people needed and wanted. We needed a business plan, start-up money... we needed everything. How were we going to do this?"

Linda thought about their young son, Andy. "We had this little guy. Was it fair to him to commit the time a brand new business required? I was scared. We had a nice nest egg, and we had worked and created a lot of wonderful things in our life, assets, and now it was a matter of letting all that go, selling everything, re-mortgaging our home, but the more I thought about it, the more I thought, 'You know, we've had success, and this has given us such a wonderful lifestyle and good growing experiences. Did you ever think, Linda, that maybe these things were happening because this was a plan for you – to learn and grow, because this was what you were meant to do? Maybe you needed all those experiences, all the good, all the not so good, to teach you the right thing to do and what you should not do.

"'Because when you were working with all those CEOs and investors as the naïve new kid on the block, and you saw how they operated, you learned a lot. You saw what worked and what did not work, and you were on this journey, because maybe it was supposed to take you to a new place.' So then I started thinking that way. You know, you have to change your thinking. Then I thought, 'Okay, let's give it a go, because we can always sell out and go to Arizona and open a sub shop, if this doesn't work.'"

We've Been Preparing For This All Our Lives

It was as if Linda and Brian Kaminski were preparing for this their entire lives – their own products, containing the natural ingredients they believed to be best for one's health and skin; a company they could call their own, one that placed the needs and desires of the independent Consultant first; and a business opportunity based on honesty and integrity. From the start, they were determined to maintain complete control of their new company and not be answerable to outside investors. Based on their experiences, they knew investors were only interested in the bottom line, and that was not always what was best for the company or its field sales force of independent distributors. "At our company, we wanted P&L to stand for People and Love and not Profit and Loss," Linda says emphatically.

Adds Brian, "Our products had to be of exceptional quality and yet affordable. We wanted to focus on helping people live a positive and healthy lifestyle."

For years, they called their "company within a company" of independent distributors L'Bri, a combination of their first names: Linda and Brian. As far back as 1984, they incorporated as L'Bri Health and Beauty, Inc. When this entrepreneurial couple worked as distributors for the two different companies and then was on staff for one of them, they continued to operate as L'Bri. Explains Brian, "The checks went to L'Bri, and then L'Bri wrote Linda and Brian payroll checks."

If the parent company did not offer a product the Kaminskis believed in, such as aloe vera, they did not hesitate to stock it themselves for their customers. "We added a few products to the line, which is unusual for direct sellers, but these were products we wanted our customers to try," says Brian. These offerings, including the aloe, were considered "private label" products, meaning Linda and Brian purchased them from a manufacturer, who applied their L'Bri label to the packaging.

"We were by no means the most successful direct sellers in the industry," Brian relates, pointing to the success stories of direct sellers earning more than $300,000 a year. "We knew we weren't the top producers in the world of direct selling," he adds. But they knew direct selling. They knew what their customers wanted and needed. They were experienced business owners. They were ready to take L'Bri to a new level of success.

We Want To Do Something With Aloe

Their experience with aloe vera, dating from Brian's wedding trip sunburn and Uncle Leo's home remedy to Brian's amazing recovery years later from the horrible burns suffered in the foundry accident, convinced them aloe would be the primary ingredient in whatever they decided to do with their new company. Brian and Linda booked a flight to the manufacturer that supplied them with the private label aloe product. "It was the place we purchased from for years," Brian explains. "We went to see them and expressed our intentions. 'We want to start our own company. Please help us develop an outstanding product line. I know we love aloe. We want to do something with aloe.'"

Most skin care products begin with water. It's the basic ingredient. Brian and Linda asked the simple question: Instead of water, can we use aloe as the basic ingredient? As it turned out, aloe vera was an excellent choice. Containing seventy-five nutrients, two hundred active compounds, twenty essential minerals, eighteen amino acids, and twelve vitamins, the liquid squeezed from the Aloe Vera Barbadensis Miller plant had been used as a healing agent since ancient times. Nicknamed "the burn plant," aloe vera was the subject of numerous scientific inquiries.

With the selection of aloe vera, Linda and Brian asked another question: Why not have all natural ingredients? No artificial scents or colors. No waxes. No oils. No artificial enhancers of any kind.

They wanted skin care formulas better than anything then on the market, whether from a direct selling company or in a department store. "Our formulas had to be so superior, they would promote healing and truly help people have younger, softer, healthier skin."

At that time, Brian says, there were a few aloe-based products, "but we wanted to go well beyond what these other people had done." Linda agrees, "We wanted to find a product developer to unite with us in our mission to offer our customers exceptional ingredients that help people have healthier skin."

The company, based in the southwestern United States near the Rio Grande Valley where aloe is grown, was enthusiastic, but Brian and Linda harbored doubts. The company was not counted among the large, full-service laboratories. Could they develop the range of products L'Bri needed?

Let's Go To A Big Company With Our Big Ideas

One of the largest custom manufacturers of skin care and cosmetics products was located in New England. "We met with the staff and chemists, and told them about our ideas to use only quality ingredients. We wanted a product that would perform," Linda recalls. The chemists looked around the conference table incredulously. "The lead chemist chuckled," she remembers the meeting. "Then he told us the perception of quality is in the mind of the consumer, saying, 'If people think a product will work, it will perform.' He told us we need not be concerned about quality. He recommended placing our effort into the marketing and not investing our money in the quality of the product. 'If the marketing is good, people will buy it,' he told us. I couldn't believe the things he was saying. Of course, we want people to purchase our products, but we want them to love the product, see results, and come back.

"We left that meeting frustrated and disillusioned," Linda says. "How could the quality of the product not matter? For us, quality was critical."

The search continued. Next stop was a custom manufacturer located in the southern states. "They told us natural ingredients were more expensive and we could use alternatives that were less costly, but still provide results,"

Linda explains. "They were willing to help us, but I felt they were not one hundred percent on board with our concept. I wanted a team that was excited about coming out with products that were natural, really special in the marketplace, and that would be the very best for our customers. I thought they looked at us as just another account."

Next stop, a company in the Midwest. "Again, they said we were too focused on quality, and our insistence on using pharmaceutical-grade ingredients was unrealistic," Linda says. "Most companies rely on cosmetic-grade formulations, and that is sufficient according to government standards developed by the Food and Drug Administration. Just because cosmetic-grade is acceptable doesn't necessarily mean it's the best. We wanted the best of the best for our products. We wanted pharmaceutical-grade ingredients."

Linda and Brian flew to New York to meet with still another manufacturer. "The staff at this laboratory recommended developing products that are on trend," Linda remembers. "We listened. We understand that marketing is important, but the best marketing is word-of-mouth. If we can get people to try our superior products, they will tell their friends, and we will be successful."

According to Brian, manufacturers wanted to work with them, but did not necessarily buy into the idea of relying on natural ingredients that truly enhance healthy skin. "Some of the chemists recommended we add trace amounts of ingredients, such as Vitamin C, that are known to do wonders for the skin, just so we could list them on the label. In reality, these trace amounts would be ineffective and serve only to confuse the consumer," he says. "We wanted to use natural, beneficial ingredients in amounts that would make a difference for people, not just be window dressing for the label."

Brian admits many of these manufacturers had a point. "There are billions of dollars in products sold every year, from companies much larger than ours, that focus on marketing, packaging, and trends, rather than on ingredients."

Adds Linda, "There are products where the packaging costs more to manufacture than what is in the bottle. The experts told us to design products that are adequate, that look nice, and they will sell. We did not want L'Bri to be one of those companies. We didn't want to settle for adequate."

After months of research and interviewing a number of large, custom manufacturers, Linda and Brian returned to the small, aloe vera-specialty company in the southwest. Believing in Linda and Brian, the company put together a team of chemists committed to bringing quality aloe-based products to market.

"The chemists in the lab guided us in our work, steering away from petrochemicals, waxes, and oils," says Brian. "We made sure everything we used was well within FDA regulations and was documented to be healthy for the skin."

One particular chemist carefully listened to Brian and Linda's requirements. "He caught my vision," Linda says. "No artificial coloring. Nothing that does not promote healing and health. I really wanted a product that was going to perform." There was another requirement. Linda and Brian insisted that any research and development could not involve testing on animals.

Today, Linda refers to these amazing chemists as her "Team of Excellence."

How Much Is This Going To Cost?

The chemists and laboratory assistants went to work to create a comprehensive skin care line of cleansers and moisturizers, but the price tag would be high. They estimated the research and development alone could require months, possibly as long as a year.

The task ahead was daunting. Linda and Brian needed money. A lot of money. "It seemed every time we turned around, there was something else – we needed a marketing plan, a basic training manual, legal fees, all the things it takes to start a company," Brian remembers.

They made an appointment with their bank and mortgaged the house, but it was not enough. They met with the Small Business Administration, but the red tape and paperwork required seemed overwhelming. "Two hundred forms to fill out, and the interest was ten percent for an SBA loan," Brian says. "All the while, we're getting credit card offers in the mail. 'We'll give you $20,000 right now for an introductory rate of six percent for nine months,'" Brian recalls the solicitations that arrived daily in their mailbox. They ended up borrowing $150,000 on credit cards alone.

As the cash flowed to cover R&D and other start-up costs, Linda and Brian depleted their savings. It was still not enough.

Now the credit cards were coming due. Brian hunted for "deals" and opened more credit card accounts, borrowing cash needed to pay older accounts charging higher interest rates. "We borrowed $20,000 from American Express, $30,000 from MBNA, $15,000 from CitiBank, and on and on. We borrowed from one card to pay the balance on another card. We played that game for several years. In the end, we got that money for six or seven percent for the entire time we needed it, versus the higher rate of an SBA loan."

To Stay Afloat, Sell The Boat

By then, Brian and Linda were in too deep to pull out. They had to see this through. They began selling their possessions. The first to go on the block was their 20-foot-long boat. The Hurricane Deck boat with a 200 horse-power outboard motor sold for $12,000. The family loved that boat, especially six-year-old Andy.

"It was a beautiful boat," Linda says. "Only a year old, so it was brand new. One of the things our family enjoyed for relaxation was boating."

Linda and Brian's 20-foot Hurricane Deck boat is one of the many possessions sold to help finance the start-up of their company, L'Bri Pure n' Natural.

As the boat was hauled away, Andy asked his mother, "Mom, when are we going to have our boat?" Linda promised, "In two years, when you are eight years old, we'll have a boat again." At that point, with no money in the bank and thousands of dollars in debt, Linda remembers thinking, "How are we going to do this? A boat is not something that should be first on our list of priorities."

It was tough to see the boat go.

Boxes upon boxes of L'Bri products, specifically formulated with aloe to Brian and Linda's specifications, began arriving at their home. It was nearly a daily occurrence. A UPS truck or motor freight semi-trailer rumbled up the suburban street, stopping in front of the Kaminski house to unload cartons of facial creams, moisturizers, and cleansers, all bearing the L'Bri logo. Crammed full, the basement storeroom overflowed into the living room and then the hallway.

The Best Hand & Body Lotion Money Can Buy

"We now had the basic product line," Brian says in an enthusiastic voice, "plus some glamour items, and our business started to take off. We sold some product and shipped merchandise out of the basement. Linda was pounding the streets, sampling people, selling product, sponsoring people, and training Consultants. We decided we needed to add an excellent hand and body lotion to the line, because that's a staple product," Brian explains. Unfortunately, the bank account was empty. Credit cards were maxed out. They had one more asset: Brian's Lexus luxury automobile. "I asked our neighbor if we sold our car, could we borrow his car once in awhile to get us through," Brian recalls. The neighbor agreed. Placing an advertisement in the newspaper, the couple sold the Lexus, receiving just enough to develop the formula and then manufacture several thousand bottles of L'Bri Daily Moisturizing Hand & Body Lotion, made with aloe.

Explains Brian, "We personally really had to cut back on our lifestyle for a couple years, and that was okay. We could see the light at the end of the tunnel. We were totally confident from day one that this would be a success, a good company for a lot of people."

Selling the Lexus was an excellent sacrifice. After all, the new L'Bri Hand & Body Lotion contained aloe and forty-one other quality ingredients such as vitamins, natural botanicals, Echinacea extract, ginseng extract, and cucumber essence, making it one of the best, if not the best, product of its kind on the market.

The cost was high, but Linda and Brian agreed it was

well worth the investment. "Everyone loved it and told us it was the best they ever tried," says Linda. Today, L'Bri Hand & Body Lotion is consistently among the company's top sellers.

When they needed a car, Linda and Brian telephoned their neighbors, Ken and Theresa, who were retired. Their car was often available during the day, and if not, another neighbor was willing to have her car serve as back up.

"It was pretty humbling," Brian says, "a 40-year-old guy who was driving a Lexus is now borrowing the neighbor's car."

Soon after selling the Lexus, Brian called Ken. "May I borrow your car this morning?" He drove to Wal-Mart and purchased a bicycle for $79. "Now I rode the bike to get around town and run errands," Brian says.

I Know, Let's Have A Garage Sale

There was not enough money to hire employees, but Linda and Brian received help and encouragement from those closest to them. For example, Brian's father, Tony, came to the house to stuff envelopes, address circulars and postcards, and contribute another set of hands.

Despite the volunteer assistance, cash continued to be in short supply. Linda suggested they hold a garage sale. They went through the house and decided which pieces of furniture they could get along without. A redwood picnic table on the patio was not a necessity, along with lamps, chairs, framed artwork, their snow skis, floats and fishing gear, older coats and sweaters, clothes and toys Andy had outgrown, and kitchen utensils, glassware, and dishes. "Since we operated a business in the home, we could process bank cards," Brian says. "Putting up a sign that read, 'MasterCard and Visa Accepted' made our sale a little different than most."

A lady parked her car at the curb and walked up the

sidewalk. Spying the redwood picnic table and then "MasterCard/Visa Accepted" sign, she had to laugh. As Brian remembers the incident, "She thought that sign was really a hoot. Then I said, 'We offer free delivery' and got out my appointment book. 'Okay, what day's good for you?' My appointment book was this incentive gift we were giving to our Consultants."

The faux leather woman's day planner caught the lady's attention. She asked Brian, "Whoa, where did you get that?" To which Brian explained that he and Linda owned L'Bri Pure n' Natural, and the day planner was an incentive gift available only to L'Bri Consultants.

"Can I get one from you?" the lady asked hopefully. "Come on," she begged. "I'll give you twenty dollars for it." Brian stood his ground: "No, I can't do that. People are working for these. I just can't give them away or sell them."

Overhearing the pleading, Linda stepped in and offered to give the lady some L'Bri samples. Weeks later, after trying the samples, the lady asked to become a L'Bri Consultant. She earned the day planner and today is one of the company's top achievers, earning more than $100,000 a year. By the way, on the day of the garage sale she purchased the redwood picnic table. Brian borrowed a friend's truck and delivered it to her home.

It was Linda and Brian's first and last garage sale. "Whatever we could think of that was no longer a necessity, we got rid of," Linda says. They raised nearly two thousand dollars.

Linda no longer shopped for new outfits, shoes, and purses. Until now, she always planted lots of spring and summer annuals around the house. The flowers went on hold. They cut back on the weekly grocery bill by making do with less. As Linda says, "We didn't waste a thing."

If You Try It, You Will Like It

Later, Linda and Brian leased a Toyota for $190 a month plus tax, so Linda could continue the business by conducting facial classes, meeting with potential Consultants, and giving samples. As it turned out, sampling was to be the road out of debt – and out of the basement.

The new hand and body lotion was a superior product, and people loved it, if they tried it. Trial was the key. The Kaminskis purchased thousands of plastic half-ounce bottles and using a funnel, Brian meticulously began filling each half-ounce bottle with a little hand and body lotion. After several hundred of these, he says, "I got wise." He adapted a Wagner power painter/sprayer to be a bottle-filling machine. "We ordered the hand and body lotion in gallon jugs, and I stuck a plastic tube in the gallon jug and used the Wagner painter/sprayer. It was really high tech," he laughs about the Rube Goldberg device rigged up in a corner of the basement. "Then we labeled the bottles. Andy helped put on the labels. They were put on crooked a lot of times." They made more than 5,000 hand and body lotion samples.

"The Wal-Mart parking lot was a real good spot" for giving away samples, Linda remembers with enthusiasm. "At this point, we had mortgaged the farm, so to speak. The business was now about survival. My greatest inspiration to really get out there and make this work in a quick way was Andy," she explains. "We had a family. So I was on a mission."

Wal-Mart was a sampling nirvana. Linda dressed in a business suit. "If you look too casual, your prospects are not going to take you seriously," she advises.

"I positioned my car so I could see people coming out the door. I would see women coming out of the store pushing their shopping carts. It was perfect, because when they opened the door or trunk of their car, I made my approach. They were no longer shopping and so were receptive to listen. I walked up and said, 'Excuse me, can I get your opinion on something?' That's how I started my approach. 'I'm working with a brand new line of pure and natural products called L'Bri Pure n' Natural. Have you heard of them, yet?' Of course, they said no. I continued, 'I'm looking for people who would enjoy trying pure and natural products, and I would love to treat you to a free sample. Would you enjoy trying a free sample and then giving me your name and number so I can get your opinion on the product?' That was what I did. I went out and sampled people. Got names and phone numbers, and called back in two to three days to ask their opinion. I remember one woman was using an over-the-counter brand and I gave her a sample of our product. This was on a Tuesday. That Friday, she phoned me and said, 'Oh, I love these products. I have to have them right away.' I offered to ship them right out. She said, 'No, no, no. I want to come and get them now.'"

A number of potential customers, such as this lady, drove to the Kaminski home to purchase more L'Bri products. Many more placed orders, especially when Linda called to follow up on her "survey." Most became long-time L'Bri devotees.

We Hit A Home Run Here

"We knew we hit a home run," Linda exclaims. Visiting retirement communities, she gave away hand and body lotion samples. "We had one elderly woman in a wheelchair who had been on psoriasis medication for years and had a severe case of it behind her knees. I suggested the body lotion, just thinking it would be soothing, not thinking anything more than that. After about two weeks, I followed up with her. She said, 'You know, my psoriasis is clearing up.' Eight or so weeks using the lotion, it was gone, totally gone. And here was a woman who was on medications for ten years. So when she went to her doctor, he said, 'Just a coincidence. You're probably in remission.' But to this day her psoriasis is gone, and it has now been eight years." The elderly woman's daughter became a L'Bri Consultant and now recommends L'Bri products made of aloe to her many customers.

More than half of the Wal-Mart customers Linda "surveyed," accepted the free samples. Brian was amazed that anyone accepted them "because of the crooked labels on some of the bottles. I'm sure a few people went home and took a look at our samples and thought this was a hokey deal. 'What? Do you make these in your basement and have a six-year old put on the labels?' Yes, we did."

Linda continues, "That doesn't mean I didn't get no's, but I learned after awhile when I got a no, instead of saying, 'Okay, well, thank you, anyway,' I gave them my brochure, and said, 'I respect your honesty, but you know what? I'll just give you my brochure, and if you ever change your mind, and feel you would like to try some Pure n' Natural skin care products, my name and number are right here on the back, and you can always contact me. I'll be more than happy to send you free samples, because I can promise you one thing: Once you try L'Bri, you'll never want to put anything else on your skin.' That leaves them with a powerful statement they will remember.

"Many of these people later called and told me, 'I keep thinking about what you said, and I want to try these samples to see if they're as good as you say they are.'"

People Are Talking And Business Is Growing

Giving away samples in the Wal-Mart parking lot, at the grocery, in office buildings, and at the mall, Linda's business began to grow. These customers told friends and co-workers about the amazing L'Bri products made with aloe. "You get fifteen people talking about your products, and these women have a network," Linda says. "They have their co-workers, their neighbors, sisters, and they start talking, and, boom, you have a business going."

Linda continues to give away samples and teaches L'Bri Consultants to do the same. "I teach our Consultants, if someone seems disinterested, or you get the feeling they're really not going to use the samples, have enough respect for yourself and ask for the sample back. Simply say, 'You know, if you don't think you're going to use these samples, please let me know now, because I do invest in them, and that way I can give them to someone else.' Many times they will say, 'I'm not interested,' or they'll reply, 'No, no, no, I'll try them.' At least they know you're serious."

According to Linda Kaminski, "There's a right way to sample, and there's a wrong way to sample." If you do it the right way, the potential customer is intrigued to try the product, and the Consultant comes away with the contact information, such as name and phone number, needed to follow up and hopefully get an order.

"Everyone wants to look and feel young," she says. "And people are looking for natural products that don't contain harmful chemicals. We have a superb product, at the right time, and we're affordable." To date, the L'Bri company has given away samples by the hundreds of thousands, and there is every indication this number will continue to climb. On a daily basis, potential customers from throughout the United States hear about L'Bri Pure n' Natural and log on to the internet to request free samples.

At www.lbri.net/samples, visitors complete a simple questionnaire, agree to pay a nominal fee to cover shipping and handling, and request free samples of cleanser, freshener, and moisturizer packaged as the Customized Skin Care Trio; a sample of Smooth n' Firm Eye Repair Gel; a Facial Masque; the Rejuvenating Enzyme Facial Peel; and the famous L'Bri Moisturizing Hand & Body Lotion. Samples provide a week to 10-day trial of the products.

"When you're able to offer samples to people, you're saying to them, 'My product is so good, and I believe in it so much that I want to give you a free sample to try,'" Linda explains. "Handing out samples and following up with prospects launched our company."

We Need To Move The Business, But Where?

Eighteen months following the arrival of the first shipments of L'Bri products, the Kaminski house was bursting at the seams. There was simply no more room to accommodate the growing company. Climbing aboard his bicycle, Brian pedaled off in search of an office with an attached warehouse. He figured it needed to be relatively close to home, so he could get there on his bike. Riding along Holz Parkway, past Miniwaukan Park, he crossed a river and turned onto Perkins Drive and a small industrial park. There he found their new home office. The building was actually a series of offices and warehouses, rented by the unit. One unit, on the south end, was available. At 2,500 square feet, it offered a meeting room, three offices, and an adjoining warehouse.

"That was a big jump for us, going from the house to this," Brian relates, but there was just enough cash flow to cover the monthly rent and utilities. Brian and Linda signed the paperwork. The company had yet to turn a profit, but as Linda puts it, "We were constantly improving." They upgraded the printing of the L'Bri sales catalog. More Consultants joined the company.

Brian was out of bed at 4:00 a.m. "We had a lot of good things happening," he recalls. "Customers were loving the products. Consultants were making money. The company was growing. It was tough to sleep."

Linda says her husband, putting in twenty-hour days,

seven days a week "was running on adrenalin." Finally, after nearly two years of seeing Brian work around the clock, Linda said enough was enough. "It was ridiculous. He was up at 4 a.m., worked until midnight or 1:00 a.m., every day of the week, including Saturday and Sunday. I finally said, 'This has got to stop.'" She told Brian he could not get out of bed until 6:00 a.m.

He continued to go to the office on weekends. "It was all good," he says of the business. "So much was happening, it was easy to come in on Saturday and Sunday."

While Brian burned the midnight oil, Linda was keeping pace with him. She remembers, "There were times I was on the phone talking so much, I lost my voice from the strain."

Customers Come Back For More

As in the days with Viviane Woodard and Finelle, the Kaminskis emphasized repeat business. They reasoned, it was easy to keep a customer who was happy with your service as well as the product. Brian was on the phone, following up with long-time customers. "How are you doing?" "How do you like the products?" He mailed thank-you cards, sent sale flyers, stayed in touch.

The on-the-job education gleaned from years of operating "a business within a business" kicked in. "All the time we worked with the other companies, I guess we were learning the ropes about how to run a business," Brian says. "Little things like how to process credit card payments and larger things such as creating a newsletter, printing catalogs, operating a shipping department, and issuing commission checks to the independent sales force. I was always asking, 'How do you do that?' 'How does this work?' 'Who does that sort of thing?' I was always asking questions and learning, not thinking of doing my own thing, just being nosey," Brian says. Now all this knowledge was paying dividends.

Andy Becomes A Cucumber Tycoon

From the time he was old enough to help with the business, Andy pitched in. Brian says their son "was always asking, 'What can I do?'" Label the sample bottles, stuff envelopes, and staple packets together. Observing his parents operate an on-going business in the home, Andy became "very entrepreneurial."

"When he was about six years old, we had an overabundance of cucumbers in the garden," Linda remembers one particular summer day. "We had so many cucumbers, they were going to waste. So I suggested to Andy and his little friend, Amanda, 'Why don't you and Amanda load up the coaster wagon and take the cucumbers to the neighbors next door and across the street, and give them away?'

"I saw them in the garden loading up the wagon and then about twenty minutes went by, and I went outside to look for them, and they were nowhere to be found. Andy knew he wasn't permitted to leave a certain boundary. I went next door to Theresa's house. 'Was Andy here? Did you see him?'

"'Yes, he was here,' Theresa told me. 'I bought some cucumbers from him.' I said, 'You bought some cucumbers?' She said, 'Sure did, a buck apiece.' In the summer you know how inexpensive cucumbers are. 'Theresa, he wasn't supposed to sell them. He was supposed to give them away.'

'Oh, no,' she said, 'we bought.' So then I went across the street, the same thing. The lady across the street bought the cucumbers at a buck apiece; next door, same thing, a buck apiece. He was nowhere to be found. So now I was out in the subdivision, and all of a sudden there he was with his coaster wagon almost empty, and he had a fistful of money! Selling! Six years old, and he had eight dollars in his hand. I said, 'What are you doing?' He said, 'I'm selling cucumbers. Look! Look!' He was all excited. I said, 'Honey, you were supposed to give them away.' He looked up at me and said, 'They needed cucumbers. They bought them, Mom. They bought them.'

"I was just astounded. Nowhere did we implant that idea, nowhere. Then I was left with what to do as a parent. What was the right thing to do? Do I make him give the money back to the people? So Brian and I had this discussion. What do we do? This was not right. He wasn't supposed to sell them. But then we thought, 'You know, he wasn't supposed to sell them, that was true, but they didn't have to buy them, either.'

"Later that night, I remember thinking, 'Well, good for him.' You know, he asked, and he got, and isn't that what we say about life? You have to ask. If you don't ask, how can you get? We allowed him to keep the money."

Growing Up In The Business

Growing up in the family business, it became second nature for Andy to establish personal goals and work to make those goals a reality. Says Linda, "When I was young, I had no self-confidence, but Andy is self-assured and very much a positive thinker. I didn't learn anything about goal setting until I was somewhere in my twenties. No one ever talked to me about goal setting and the importance of it. He has an entirely different way of thinking, because he's with parents that are looking and talking about things differently. We're always talking about setting goals and writing them down. He's a list maker now. He's just doing so many things that we didn't do until we were in our late twenties, and to me, that's so incredibly rewarding.

"Some of the things that come out of his mouth are amazing. We look at each other, and Brian will say, 'My work is done,' because we never thought that way at his age.

"He's a very responsible young man. He's not so much a follower. He's a leader."

At age fifteen and looking forward to ninth grade, Andy surprised his parents with a request: to be enrolled at St. John's Northwestern Military Academy. Located in Delafield, Wisconsin, the prestigious St. John's Military Academy was founded in 1884 and boasts a number of influential alumni including several generals, admirals, corporate CEOs, ambassadors, and members of Congress. The boarding school is twenty minutes from the Kaminski home.

For two previous summers, Andy attended week-long summer camps at the school. "They did rafting, the obstacle course, and archery; so, of course, it was a boy's world, and he loved it," his mother says. When Andy announced he would like to attend St. John's, Linda and Brian attempted to discourage the idea. They pointed out the strict code of conduct, the mandatory study hours, no television, no iPods, that he would be away from home and his friends.

Andy was not discouraged and continued to lobby for St. John's. His parents "tried to talk him out of it," resorting to bribery, including a thousand-dollar paint ball gun and the promise to set aside cash for a new car when he turned twenty-one. Nothing worked.

When Linda asked their son why he was so determined to go away to school at St. John's, Andy told his mother: "I just really think it would help me in my life. I really want this experience."

A few weeks later, Andy said he wanted to attend the military school because "I want to get a jump start on life." Brian and Linda relented and enrolled their son at St. John's.

They knew life at St. John's was strict, but after Andy's first weeks at the school, they learned just how strict life could be: the shined shoes and scrubbed rooms. "Your bed must be made perfectly," Brian points out. "You can't even sit on your bed. They don't give you a mattress pad cover. You have to earn that."

Currently enrolled at the school, Andy has earned promotions in rank and maintains some of the highest scores in his class of 325 cadets. He excels in basketball and baseball and was accepted to the St. John's cross-country team. He runs four miles a day.

Brian marvels that their son gave up his comfortable room at home for "what amounts to a jail cell" at the military academy. "But Andy knows that hugely successful people have come out of that school. Not to say that everybody that comes out of there is going to be super successful, but one hundred percent of them for the last one hundred years have gone on to college. There's never been one child that went through the school that did not go."

"You can pretty much pick your college, and you'll get in if you say you're from Saint John's," Linda adds proudly. "Whether he stays there throughout his entire high school experience, I don't know, but it wasn't something that we pushed on him at all. If anything, we discouraged him and his friends discouraged him from going."

Loyalty, Responsibility, And That Family Feeling

Loyalty and responsibility are two concepts dear to Brian and Linda's collective hearts. Says Brian, "We have a huge feeling of responsibility to our Consultants because of what we went through when Linda was an independent Beauty Advisor with other companies. We want to make sure our independent L'Bri Consultants are secure with us, can depend on us, and will have the confidence they will always have a solid home with our company. We want to do the right thing for our Consultants. They're like our family. We want to make sure we give them a happy home for the rest of their lives."

This commitment to their independent Consultants, both the long-term ones and those that continue to join the company everyday, is born of Linda and Brian's direct selling experiences. Says Linda, "There's nothing worse than putting your heart and soul into something and then having other people, with not the right intentions, come in and destroy your dream. That happened to us twice. We will not let that happen at L'Bri."

"You can imagine how sensitive we are about back orders and making sure bonus checks are always mailed on time," Brian explains. "We might have had one color of lipstick on back order for a week or two, but there has never been an actual, real back order of a product, and there has never been a late commission check. In fact, we are so sensitive about that, we send out checks on the fifteenth of every month, and if the fifteenth is on a Saturday or Sunday, we send the checks out on Friday."

A long-time L'Bri Pure n' Natural employee, Dawn Knapmiller, is the company's shipping manager.

*Today, Kathy Wisniewski is Linda's executive assistant.
She has been working with Linda since 1981, the year
she became an independent Beauty Advisor.*

Loyalty Is A Two-Way Street

At L'Bri, loyalty is a two-way street that spans the
years. Dawn Knapmiller was helping Brian set up the telephone system when the company relocated to Perkins
Drive. Efficient, personable, and a quick study, Dawn was
the ideal choice, if Brian and Linda needed an all-around
"Jill-of-all-trades" employee. It was soon apparent that
they needed such a utility player, and Dawn was offered the
job. "In no time, Dawn was filling and packing orders, issuing invoices, working with our Consultants to answer
their questions, doing it all," says Brian. That was in 1999.
Today, she is L'Bri's shipping manager.

Kathy Wisniewski joined Linda's Viviane Woodard
team as one of her first Beauty Advisors in 1981. She followed Linda to Finelle, back to Viviane Woodard, and then
became a top manager with L'Bri. A few years ago, Linda

realized, "I needed someone I could really trust and count on to help us here in the office." She considered several candidates, but wanted Kathy. "I totally trust her with everything," Linda explains. At Linda's urging, Kathy left field sales and now is a member of the L'Bri corporate staff, serving as Linda's executive assistant.

We Love Our Suppliers And They Like Us, Too

This sensitivity to loyalty and responsibility carries over to L'Bri's many vendors, the companies that manufacture their products, print the catalogs, provide website design services, or any of a myriad of other services needed by a growing concern. Most vendors extend sixty to ninety days of credit, and they offer the same to L'Bri, however, Brian and Linda pay the bills immediately. "Our vendors tell us we're the best paying customers they have," Brian says proudly. "We pay invoices within a few days after receiving them."

As one vendor recently told Brian, "You're not our biggest customer, but you're the best paying customer."

This reputation for paying quickly has its advantages. One holiday season, L'Bri needed a large order in time for Christmas deliveries. Brian called the vendor to see what could be done to accommodate the abbreviated schedule. Jobs placed by other companies went to the back burner, and the L'Bri order became the immediate priority.

"Our obsession with paying bills right away wasn't done with that plan in mind," Brian says. "It just turned out that way."

Paying the bills quickly is only one of many ways Brian and Linda express their gratitude. For some of their largest suppliers, the Kaminskis sponsor annual holiday parties for the employees, treating everyone to Christmas lunch. It's not unusual for a long-time vendor to receive a restaurant gift certificate as a "thank you" or a department store gift card for a job well done.

Says Linda, "You need to be appreciative of the people that are helping you. We believe that's important."

A Bicycle Has Its Rewards And A Few Challenges

With Linda driving the car to Wal-Mart and other locations to give away samples, Brian continued to pedal his bicycle in the morning the three miles to the office and in the evening the three miles home. At some points, the road narrowed to not much more than a country lane. It was excellent exercise, helping to keep Brian thin and fit, but riding a bike can have its challenges, especially in the months of a harsh Wisconsin winter.

More than once, a passing motorist drenched him with flying slush. "Sometimes the county snow plow only cleared one lane for traffic, so it was a little tricky," Brian says. "There was a bridge and in the winter, only two cars could go over at a time. If there was a fair amount of traffic, I had to pull over and wait for the cars to go by. Occasionally, one of my neighbors would see me riding my bike, and I felt kind of silly," Brian admits. At times, he felt sorry for himself, but would quickly shake that "woe is me" attitude, because "I knew riding the bike was temporary."

On one particular evening, with the temperature below zero, Brian made his way through the cutting wind, arriving home well after nightfall. Propping the bike along the garage wall, he struggled into the house, flopped into a chair, and sighed, "What have we got ourselves into?"

Help! We Need More Room

The company was outgrowing the 2,500 square foot office/warehouse space, and Brian was concerned. It was time to find a larger space. Then the tenant next door moved out. Brian leased the second unit, doubling the space to 5,000 square feet. About a year later, "we were growing and bursting at the seams again, and I didn't know quite what to do," Brian explains. "We were looking at other warehouses, and all of a sudden another tenant moved out. Wow, perfect. We took over another 2,500 square feet; growing, growing, building, growing, bursting at the seams, back out looking for a warehouse. Guess what? The last tenant in the building moved out. Boom, we had 10,000 square feet, the entire structure."

Brian and Linda plan to either build or purchase an even larger building and are considering adding a second and third shift to the shipping department. "One of our service goals is to ship products immediately. An order received today ships to the customer no later than tomorrow. Our customers are very happy with the quick service we provide as a matter of course," says Brian.

Linda & Brian Kaminski

6: WHERE WE GO FROM HERE

Built On Trust And Honesty

From the beginning, this husband and wife worked together as a team. "I think for any relationship to work long-term, there has to be a deep level of trust and honesty," Linda says. "If I didn't have the utmost feeling that I could trust Brian and count on him, then none of this would have worked."

Along with trust and honesty, a third ingredient to their success has been ambition. "We saw the light and the opportunity inherent in this type of business at the same time," Brian says. "We set similar goals and were not afraid to work and put in the hours. I guess we were lucky to find each other and believe in the same things."

"We always wanted to see where this journey would take us and travel to the next spot together," Linda adds.

"When people learn we have been married for thirty years and worked together nearly as many years, they can't believe it," Brian says with a broad smile. "They say, 'I could never work with my spouse and hope to stay married.' Linda and I share the same dreams and ambitions. We're life partners as well as business partners, and for us, that's the best of everything."

Hey, I Know You

After nearly thirty years in the business, Linda continues to serve a number of long-time customers and now is the trusted beauty Consultant for their children, who have grown into adulthood. "I would go to parties and do shows," Linda says. "Their kids were little, and now they are adults, and are buying L'Bri products."

A few months ago, Linda was on an airline flight originating from Chicago when the flight attendant did a double take. "Are you Linda?" she asked. "You used to come to my house, and my mom would buy from you."

Linda was amazed. "I don't know how on earth she could have recognized me, because she was young, maybe eight years old, but her mother was a client and still uses the products."

On another occasion, Brian and Linda were on vacation in Jamaica. "I was on the beach, and a woman came up and said, 'Linda, what are you doing here?' It was a customer. It was amazing."

Computer Problem? This Is Our Lucky Day

Then there's just plain old luck, such as the time Tony came into their lives. "We were setting up our software and didn't have any money," Brian recalls. "And I didn't know anything about what I was doing."

Developing a direct selling company's marketing and compensation plan is complicated. Companies may invest tens of thousands of dollars in software development. "When it came to computers, I learned Microsoft Publisher, so I could make our own flyers and pamphlets. That was about the extent of my ability," Brian admits. Wandering through the Wal-Mart computer software aisle, he struck up a conversation with another customer. "We talked for awhile, and L'Bri came up," Brian continues the story. When Brian told him he was struggling with a software issue, the man brightened and shot Brian a knowing smile.

"Oh, yeah, really?" he said. "Well, that's what I do. I'm a computer programmer and software developer. Tell you what, I'll come over and check it out for you."

"So he came to the house and fixed my problem," Brian says. "It was a hardware issue, and then Tony started teaching me about things, such as this is how DOS works, this is how you do this, and this is how you do that.

"I had my own personal computer tutor, helping me and teaching me. He was the nicest guy in the world and when I offered him money, he told me, 'No, I can't take your money.' Then I called him another time, and I said, 'Tony, you can't come over unless I pay you. I must pay you something.' So he helped me with a few more things, software issues, and he was teaching me all along, just teaching me things. He would come over for five hours on a Saturday and help me. I said, 'Okay, now how much do I owe you?'

"Tony replied, 'Just make a donation.' I wrote him a check for $150, and he mailed it back to us ripped in half."

In the months to come, Tony designed and programmed the L'Bri website and provided software programming to help with distribution, field sales compensation, and the marketing plan. He often refused payment.

As an independent programmer, Tony set his own hours. "Every time there was a computer crash or an issue, it was a big deal for us, because we couldn't get the orders processed or keep track of important information" recalls Brian. "Tony rushed right over and made it work. He took us under his wing and was happy for us. He wanted to help."

Linda says, "He just came out of the blue, because we were thinking, 'What are we going to do? We're going to have to learn all this. We're going to have to hire someone.'"

"Tony resolved our challenges and taught me along the way," Brian says. "I learned so much from him." Years later, the company was able to hire a fulltime software programmer to manage L'Bri's hardware and software. "From time to time, Tony called, stopped by, and checked in," Brian says. "We talked on the phone, and he would say, 'I came across the L'Bri name,' and he was feeling like a million bucks, because he knew he had a hand in our success."

Linda and Brian gave Tony's wife free products and sent gifts to their home, but through it all, Tony generally refused to receive money for his work. He did it simply because he wanted to help.

Another twist of luck was finding a retired programmer who enjoyed a career at Intel. An expert in designing software for direct selling companies, Ken "eats, sleeps, and drinks L'Bri," says Brian, and has committed one hundred percent of his on-the-job time to the company. "You know, I think he goes to bed with the laptop," Brian adds with a laugh. "Thanks to these two gentlemen, at L'Bri, we have one of the best software programs in the direct selling industry."

We're All About Butterflies

First-time visitors to the L'Bri corporate offices in Mukwonago initially notice two things: the friendly employees and the butterflies. In photos, drawings, displays, on posters and on the windows are pictures of butterflies. A butterfly accents the L'Bri company logo. Colorful, exotic butterflies fill a showcase mounted on the wall outside Linda's office. In short, butterflies are everywhere.

Butterflies symbolize the joy of life, happiness, and beauty. "There are wonderful poems about butterflies," Linda explains. "I love the way these poems tell the story of the butterfly. When a butterfly breaks out of the cocoon, it must struggle. Sometimes people see that happen, and they try to help the butterfly, not realizing that by helping the butterfly too much, it will come to its demise. To reach our full potential, like a butterfly, there will be challenges, and we must overcome those challenges on our own terms.

"When a butterfly opens and stretches its wings for the first time, it flies toward the light. The butterfly teaches us to come out of the dark, to free ourselves from the past, and fly to the light of a brighter tomorrow."

In the months leading to the launch of L'Bri Pure n' Natural, Linda thought about the butterfly and was considering this icon for rebirth as their company symbol. On a crisp February morning, she stepped outside the house. "As I walked, I saw a caterpillar. In February in Wisconsin, seeing a caterpillar is pretty much unheard of," she says. "'What on earth is a caterpillar doing out here at this time of year?' Then it dawned on me. This is it! Our logo must be a butterfly."

Draw Me A Treasure Map

Linda and Brian believe in "treasure maps." Not the kind pirates leave behind, but the kind of maps Linda and Brian use chart the future and establish goals worthy of their effort. You begin by posting a picture of what you want on a "vision board." It may be a Hawaiian beach scene, if you dream of flying to the islands for a vacation. It may be a drawing of a new house or a magazine clipping of a particular automobile. It may not always be materialistic. It could be the picture of good health or a happy relationship.

"The picture on the vision board is a tangible reminder to help you visualize your goals," Linda explains. "Keep this treasure map by your telephone, on the refrigerator, or wherever you see it often. When you look at that treasure map, you'll be inspired to go the extra mile and put in the effort to achieve those things that are on your treasure map."

True to her word, after the family sold their boat to keep the business afloat, Linda made a treasure map to make sure the family had a new boat within two years. "Andy remembered, because he said to me, 'I'm eight years old, Mom, and we're getting the boat now,' and we did," Linda says.

Over the years, Linda and Brian used their treasure maps and vision boards, reminding them to work harder to earn an incentive trip, or a car, or a new house. "We went to the home shows, always had pictures of new homes up and around," Brian says. "Treasure maps and vision boards were daily reminders of our goals and dreams."

Then Brian came across a picture of a Corvette, painted in sunset orange, the color of Linda's hair when they were younger. Riding the bicycle, he dreamed of someday driving the sunset orange Corvette. Today, that sunset orange Corvette can be seen parked in front of the L'Bri corporate offices.

"It's just beautiful," Brian says.

Quality Products And No Fluff

L'Bri's intensely loyal customers are convinced aloe, the primary ingredient in many of the company's most popular skin care products, heals, nurtures, softens, and keeps them looking young. As Brian tells anyone who asks, most skin care products use water as the first ingredient. Water is certainly not bad for you," he continues. "Water is okay, but aloe is better. I think everyone would agree, especially anyone who has experienced it, that aloe vera is better for your skin than water."

Next, L'Bri products rely less on chemicals and more on natural ingredients. Points out Linda, "Our products have a shorter shelf life than other products, because they're natural."

"We're very passionate about our products, that they perform, and do what we promise," Brian says. "In general, as an industry, skin care and cosmetics sell a lot of fluff, pretty packaging, sweet scents and supermodels. Consumers see the advertising and purchase products, try them, fill a drawer with them, and then years later throw them out. They may purchase something because they got a free bag at the department store or a famous model talked about it on television. It's fluff and salesmanship. At L'Bri, we talk about educating our customers so they can judge for themselves what is better for them. Which is better? Aloe or water? Which would you rather use on your skin?

"Educating our customers about oils, chemicals, artificial coloring, and artificial fragrances, we believe, is best for the long-term. People read the labels on what they eat. We want them to read the labels on what they put on their skin. We're one of the few companies that teach people how to read the labels on their skin care products. An educated customer will purchase the best products for themselves and their family."

Keep It Affordable And We'll Help More People

L'Bri products are affordable. "If we can keep our prices in line, we can reach and help more people," Linda explains. "We would rather earn less profit and help more people experience the difference aloe-based products can make for them."

As for the thousands of L'Bri independent Consultants, Linda Kaminski has been there, done that, understands their needs, acknowledges their fears, and helps them achieve success. After all, Linda has given away samples, experienced rejection, served customers, demonstrated products at home parties, and proven herself by becoming a top sales leader.

"Here you have someone who has walked the walk," Brian says, "who has been up and down, who has done presentations where no one showed, done presentations where no one purchased a thing. Linda had the challenges and had the success. So, who better to support, help and guide you than someone who has done it and truly cares?"

The Proof Is In The Doing

"Anyone can say they care about you, their products are superior, or that they have your best interest in mind," Brian says. "The proof is in the doing and the seeing."

Those who get to know this couple claim, "They're the real deal."

Unlike some companies, L'Bri ships the order directly to the customer, so Consultants need not purchase or stock inventory.

"We would rather see our independent Consultants have the time to meet with customers, present demonstrations, and talk about our products than be concerned about excessive paperwork, inventory, deliveries, and those tasks that do not generate sales," Brian says.

"That's busy work," Linda adds. "It's a necessary part of a business, but it's not the action steps that will build sales. We want our independent Consultants talking to people, sharing the products, doing presentations, taking orders, and then going home to receive a nice check in the mail for their efforts.

"We do everything we can to help our independent field sales Consultants be successful," Linda says. "That's why we constantly are implementing programs that make their journey with us even easier."

I See Happy People Living A Lifestyle

The future of L'Bri Pure n' Natural is indeed bright. Independent Consultants, learning about this amazing business opportunity from family and friends, continue to join on a daily basis. Customers are discovering the aloe-based L'Bri products, and they want more. To date, the company offers more than a hundred different products for a variety of skin types.

In 2006, Linda and Brian honored L'Bri top achievers with an all-expenses paid vacation to Las Vegas as part of the company's Founder Club incentive program. From left, Brian, Jennifer Piala, Kathy Roen, Grace Burmester, Maria Burgos, Gina LaGalbo, Linda, and Gina's husband, Tom LaGalbo. Jennifer, Kathy, Grace, Maria and Gina are executive managers within the company's field sales program.

Linda's vision of the company is expansive. "I see women from all walks of life accomplishing and achieving their goals and dreams. I see people happy. I see them living lifestyles, not just making a living, but living a lifestyle. I see them helping other people and in return being rewarded for their efforts.

"Direct selling, as an industry, is a wonderful way to achieve wealth," she adds. "Direct selling works. It is a proven business model. Find the right company for you, be a good student of the business, and then work the business. This is what L'Bri offers to anyone who is looking for more in their life."

This Business Is About More Than Making A Buck

Brian talks about the intangible benefits of being an independent L'Bri Consultant. "This kind of business gives people self-confidence, gets them thinking about having goals for their lives, and gives them the courage to do things they never considered possible. This is a business that's much more than making a buck. This is something that makes people feel better about themselves."

Linda agrees: "I stayed in direct sales, because I loved it. As an independent sales Consultant, I was my own boss. I controlled my income, decided how much I wanted to earn, and I was limited only by the amount of effort and time I wished to devote to the business."

The realization that just about anything is possible in direct sales came soon after Linda became a Viviane Woodard Beauty Advisor. "Brian and I were married just a few years, and we had no savings. We lived from paycheck to paycheck," Linda remembers. "Within a six-week period, our clothes dryer stopped working, the refrigerator gave up the ghost, and the window air conditioner quit. Most young people, like us, would have pulled out the credit card, replaced the appliances, and gone into debt, resigned to make minimum payments for years to come."

At that moment, Linda saw an opportunity to put her direct selling business to work. "I got busy, made more phone calls, talked to more people, booked more presentations, and quickly earned the money we needed. We purchased the new dryer, a refrigerator, and the air conditioner, and we paid cash.

"It felt good not to go into debt," she says. "I knew then that I truly was in charge of my livelihood."

The Business Of Life-Long Lessons

A L'Bri Pure n' Natural independent Consultant recently told Linda she received a promotion at work. "This is wonderful," Linda expressed her happiness in hearing the good news. That's when the Consultant told her: "I got the promotion, I know, because of L'Bri and what I've learned and the confidence I've gained."

Having a direct selling business, such as L'Bri, opens doors for people in all walks of life. Such a business teaches life-long lessons that lead to success. "When we were in school, no one taught us about setting goals, how to work with people, about believing in yourself," Linda observes. "We were not told how to deal with rejection or the fact that many of the most successful people in the world, such as Isaac Newton, Emily Dickinson, and Albert Einstein, at one time or another faced the rejection of their ideas.

"Direct selling taught me how not to take rejection personally, but to understand rejection is part of the journey to success," she continues. "Through my direct selling business, I developed confidence, learned to overcome a fear of speaking before large groups, and gained skills far beyond anything learned on a college campus.

"I love the fact our direct selling industry levels the playing field for so many people," says Linda. "Your background doesn't matter. Your level of education is not a factor. You are in charge of your future. That truly is security, knowing you can produce results for yourself and your family.

"In direct selling, no one can lay me off or tell me I can't be promoted. To the contrary, the more effort you put into the business, the more income is earned."

According to this high-achieving direct seller, employees in a nine-to-five job may be loyal, may work hard and be fully committed to their companies, but never receive the kinds of rewards direct selling provides. Too often, recognition is reserved for a pat on the back and a "good job, keep up the hard work."

At a company such as L'Bri Pure n' Natural, income is based on effort, and achievements are rewarded with vacations to exotic locations such as Mexico's Riviera Maya, luxury automobiles, shopping sprees, and cash bonuses.

We Love This Business

Reflecting on her career in direct selling, Linda says it is a business she loves. "Facing the difficulties we encountered over the years, first as an independent sales Consultant and later as the founders of our own company, we could have jumped ship several times, and no one would have blamed us. We pressed on, because the rewards in direct selling are unlike anything else in the world of business. Brian and I were looking for more out of life. We found it in direct sales."

On one recent morning, while walking through the busy shipping department, chatting with happy employees and watching L'Bri Pure n' Natural cartons fill UPS trucks, Brian Kaminski told a guest: "I was confident that if we worked hard, did the right things, sold a good product at a fair price with good service, we would be a success. How could it not work?"

Linda and Brian Kaminski embody the American business ideal. Working hand-in-hand as a team, they studied their trade, created products people need and want, built a company based on trust and honesty, and dared to dream that anything is possible if they applied themselves, heart, mind, and soul.

How could it not work? Indeed.

Photo by Barbara J. Slane

*Linda and Brian and their company,
L'Bri Pure n' Natural, are committed to
creating affordable aloe-based skin care
products containing natural ingredients.*

7: More About L'Bri Pure n' Natural

Linda's 12 Tips For Success In Direct Sales

1. HAVE A DREAM & KNOW WHAT YOU WANT

To be successful in any endeavor, you need a dream, and the bigger, more exciting the dream, the better. Know "why" you desire success. Then create a strategy to achieve your dream. Successful people possess the desire to be successful. They know what they want. They have a reason to devote time to the business. People lacking desire or who do not know what they want, are easily distracted. They confront an obstacle, and they give up. It puts them out of business.

2. ALWAYS HAVE A GOAL IN MIND

I never go to a presentation saying, "Oh, I hope somebody buys." I always go with a goal in mind: "I'm going to sell six hundred dollars tonight or eight hundred dollars, and I'm going to sponsor two new Consultants and have two bookings." I always go to a presentation with an expectation. Always have the attitude that people are going to buy and people are interested in what you have to offer.

3. FOLLOW UP

Often, Consultants start out doing everything right. They book presentations, give samples and meet people, but then they drop the ball, because they do not follow up. For long-term success, follow up is key. If you are not following up, why bother taking the first step? Make contacts. Contact them again, and again.

4. NEVER PREJUDGE

I remember one time a woman came to one of my

presentations, and everybody had a purse, and she walked in without a purse. So right away, I was thinking, "She doesn't have a purse; there's no wallet; she's not going to buy. She's coming here unprepared." At the end of the presentation, she pulled a credit card out of her pocket and was the highest buyer of the whole group. That experience was early in my career, but it taught me you just don't pre-judge anyone. Sometimes, the people that seem the least interested end up being your biggest buyers and greatest supporters. They're the ones that end up sending you the most business. It's amazing.

5. BEWARE OF THE DREAM STEALERS

Regardless of the many success stories attributed to direct selling businesses, there are people, with the best of intentions, who will attempt to discourage you. I call these people, "The Dream Stealers," and they are often family and close friends. If I had listened to particular members of my family and well-meaning friends, I may never have tried this business. Negative thoughts smother positive actions.

6. SELL TO HELP, NOT TO EARN

Selling is about helping another person solve a problem or fulfill a need. Don't approach selling as trying to get money out of a person. Rather, help people discover a quality product that is going to do wonderful things for their skin. I think if you go with the approach that you want to make money, it's not good. The best approach, "I've got this great new product. Have you tried it, yet?" It's not about making the sale, but the end result is a sale.

7.   KEEP A POSITIVE ATTITUDE & BELIEVE IN YOURSELF

Courage and self-confidence go hand-in-hand. They both begin with positive attitude. Think good thoughts. Believe it, and you can do it.

8. BE WILLING TO LEARN

People tend not to ask for help. Their pride gets in the way. Many people get involved in this business, and they think they will do it their way. Maybe they have been in retail sales, but this is different. You have to be willing to be a follower before you can be a leader. You have to be willing to listen and learn. Park your ego at the door. Learn from the best. A Consultant who is willing to learn says, "I want to be successful. Tell me what I need to do."

9. NEVER FEAR THE WORD "NO"

"No" is the strongest, scariest word in the language. Just two letters, and they carry the weight of the world. Some people hear "no," and they curl up and retreat. When I started getting no's, I got more determined. Okay, I'm going to get the next one. Press on, turn a "no" around. Keep going, and you will eventually hear "yes."

10. BE CONSISTENT

To be a successful L'Bri Consultant is quite simple. Give away five samples a week. Book and hold a minimum of four presentations a month, and sponsor two new Consultants a month. Do that consistently for 24 months and you will be thrilled with the growth and success of your business. You can't stroll to the goal. You have to be consistent.

11. FILL IN THE NOOKS AND CRANNIES

Everyone's schedule is so full nowadays. People are caring for children, maybe holding down fulltime and part time jobs. If you want to do this business, you can if you fill in the nooks and crannies of your day. Squeeze in a phone call while the noodles are boiling on the stove. These are quick phone calls that can really do a lot for your business.

12. DON'T LOOK FOR EXCUSES

Many people look for excuses. I can't do this because.... I can't do that because... Looking for excuses is like a disease. It's called 'excuse-itis.' This is a disease that can cripple you and your business, and it's a disease you can cure. The antidote to 'excuse-itis' is in possessing a dream you are excited about. What do you dream? What do you want? Don't look for an excuse. Look for a dream.

Natural Skin Care the L'Bri Way

Never Do Harm, Always Do Good

According to Linda Kaminski, "Many of the major cosmetic companies formulate products containing ingredients that, over time, can do more harm to the skin than good. We wanted to create an affordable skin care line made with natural ingredients that would benefit the skin. Over the years, our intent remains the same: to manufacture and market the safest skin care products in the world by using the purest of ingredients and the very best nature has to offer."

Pure and natural is not a marketing slogan, but a way of life at L'Bri. L'Bri Pure n' Natural products, and there are many of them, use aloe vera as the "base" ingredient. Of the 200 or so species of the aloe plant, Aloe Vera Barbadensis Miller, the most potent and nutritious of them all, is used in quality L'Bri products. Often termed, "nature's pharmacy," aloe vera has been studied by scientists specializing in restoring, rejuvenating, and rebuilding healthy skin.

For L'Bri products, the aloe vera is cultivated in the Rio Grande Valley and picked by hand to make sure only the purest, innermost gel of the plant is used. This clear gel undergoes a "cold stabilization" process as opposed to heat pasteurization, which tends to "cook out" many of the aloe's beneficial properties. Through cold stabilization, the aloe in L'Bri skin care products retains the plant's full potency.

As remarkable as aloe appears to be, it is only part of the L'Bri product story. L'Bri Pure n' Natural skin care products are non-comedogenic, meaning they do not clog pores. There are no mineral oils, lanolin, drying alcohols, or pore-clogging waxes that can irritate skin, no artificial colors of any kind and no synthetic fragrances. The colors seen in L'Bri products as well as the scents enjoyed by customers are derived from naturally occurring color pigments and fragrances found in botanicals.

There are no animal byproducts, and L'Bri products are never tested on animals.

A L'Bri Pure n' Natural independent Consultant can provide a complete catalog of L'Bri products, and products are presented on the company's website, www.lbri.com. Here are a few of the most popular L'Bri Pure n' Natural skin care products:

Skin Care Trio

Using a three-step program for flawless skin, L'Bri Pure n' Natural customers are taught to clean, freshen, and moisturize twice a day. Begin with the Cleanser, containing aloe vera; Vitamins A, C, and E; and natural botanical extracts. Gently massage on face and neck utilizing light, upward strokes. This cleanser strips the skin of naturally-occurring lipids and removes makeup without irritation. The aloe soothes blemishes.

Next, apply the Freshener, designed to complete the cleansing process by restoring the skin's normal pH balance. Ingredients such as aloe vera, chamomile, bee pollen, horsetail, balm mint, and hypericum stimulate circulation, refine the pores, and help prevent breakouts without relying on harsh alcohol or acetone.

In the third step, smooth the Moisture Lotion over the face and neck. This lotion, enriched with aloe vera, deep ocean sea plants, Vitamin A, and natural botanical extracts, nourishes and hydrates the skin. This lightweight lotion will not clog pores, permitting the skin to "breathe."

Facial Masque

Considered "the ultimate non-surgical facelift," this intensive deep liquid cleansing treatment, containing aloe vera, natural botanical extracts, and essential oils, clears away dead, flaky cells as it tightens and tones the 52 muscles of the face. It is often used as a "spot-treatment" to speed the healing of blemishes overnight. Botanical extracts include bladderwrack (a kind of seaweed), comfrey, and chamomile. Essential oils of lemongrass, geranium, clary sage, chamomile, and violet leaf sooth the skin and promote healing.

Exfoliating Facial & Body Scrub

Gently lifts dull surface cells and imbedded impurities from the skin without damaging delicate tissues. Recommended for all skin types. Contains aloe vera, honey, complex seaweed extracts, Vitamins A, C, and E, herbal extracts, and essential oils such as lemongrass and chamomile.

Anti-Aging Formulations

Nutrients and anti-oxidants formulated for mature or aging skin restore strength and elasticity to facial tissues. "Maxifirm Skin Renewal Complex" stimulates fiberblast cells that produce protein, converting the protein into line-smoothing collagen. Independent clinical studies show a significant increase in skin firmness of as much as 21 percent in four weeks. "Time Erase Alpha Hydroxy Slow Release Serum" accelerates the emergence of younger, healthier looking skin cells. Restores skin elasticity by stimulating the production of new collagen. Fades age spots.

Daily Moisturizing Hand & Body Lotion

Containing aloe vera and forty other ingredients, the Daily Moisturizing Hand & Body Lotion is quickly absorbed by the skin to promote healing and prevent cracking and peeling. Gentle enough for the most sensitive skin, this lotion soothes, nourishes, protects, and repairs the skin. Use as a full-body lotion. Particularly beneficial on elbows and feet.

Body Wash

Ideal for bath or shower, the Body Wash cleanses away impurities while leaving the skin soft, smooth, and refreshed. Instead of using the harsh detergent sodium laurel sulfates (SLS) often found in body wash products, the L'Bri Pure n' Natural Body Wash cleans and refreshes with chamomile, calendula, ginseng, and green tea extract. Can be used on the most sensitive skin, even a baby's.

Beauty Care Cosmetics

Over the years, L'Bri Pure n' Natural customers re-quested that the company develop a makeup foundation us-ing aloe vera as the basic ingredient. The company re-sponded with Perfect Finish Liquid Foundation, one for oily skin and another for normal to dry skin. Rounding out the skin care system, the Perfect Finish Liquid Foundation actually promotes skin health. It will not clog pores and soothes the skin throughout the day with aloe vera.

The complete Beauty Care collection includes wet or dry powder foundation, powder blush, mascara, eye-shadow, eyeliner, eyebrow pencil, lip gloss, and lipliner pencils.

Wellness & Nutrition

Nutri Aloe, a comprehensive juice drink, leads off L'Bri Pure n' Natural's line up of nutritional products. Customers swear by the drink's remarkable qualities: in-creased clarity of thought, more energy, less stress, better sleep, and a host of other benefits. Containing a proprietary blend of aloe vera, Hawaiian noni fruit, pomegranate, ginkgo biloba, grape seed extract, Japanese green tea, cran-berry extract, and more than seventy trace minerals from a myriad of plant sources, Nutri Aloe is formulated to cleanse the vital organs, strengthen the immune system, and bal-ance body chemistry. The company recommends adults consume two ounces a day as a dietary supplement.

Women's Ultra and Men's Ultra are scientifically formulated supplements to serve the nutritional needs of men and women.

Providing more than thirty vitamins, minerals, and other nutrients, these supplements nourish the circulatory, digestive, and reproductive systems while strengthening the immune system.   The supplements also contain anti-oxidants to fight off free radicals that age the body.

A Daily Fiber supplement is offered for the digestive system to prevent constipation and cleanse the colon, thought to be instrumental in the prevention of colon cancer.

IMPORTANT DATES

1957 Linda and Brian are born in Milwaukee, Wisconsin.

1972 Linda and Brian are in the ninth grade together at John Marshall High School.

1975 Linda and Brian complete high school.

1975 Linda joins the Wisconsin Nursing Home Residents' Ombudsman Program.

1975 Brian is hired at Briggs & Stratton.

1976 Linda is hired at Evinrude Motors.

1977 Linda and Brian are married.

1979 Linda meets Ruth Borum, who introduces her to direct selling and Viviane Woodard.

1981 Linda joins Viviane Woodard as a Beauty Advisor. Later that year, she leaves her job at Evinrude Motors to commit full time to her Viviane Woodard business.

1981 Linda is named the Viviane Woodard "Outstanding Newcomer of the Year."

1984 Linda achieves national "Queen of Sales" at Viviane Woodard. She repeats this honor three more times.

1984 Linda and Brian incorporate as L'Bri Health and Beauty, Inc., to operate their "business within a business."

1985 Brian suffers severe burns on the job at Briggs & Stratton. Using aloe vera to treat the burns, he returns to work within four weeks.

1985 Linda earns her first incentive trip, a vacation to Catalina Island, California.

1987 Linda and Brian fly to Hawaii for the first time. Linda earns the trip as a Viviane Woodard top achiever in sales and sponsoring. In the years to come, she earns several more incentive trips, including a second vacation in Hawaii.

1987 Linda earns her first automobile from Viviane Woodard. She earns a luxury automobile the next two years as a Viviane Woodard Beauty Advisor.

1989 Linda leaves Viviane Woodard to become a Beauty Advisor with Finelle Cosmetics.

1989 Linda and Brian lease office space for their Finelle business.

1990 Linda earns an Oldsmobile Cutlass, the first of several automobiles from Finelle. Also that year, she earns a trip to Cancun as a top Finelle achiever. In the years to come, she earns trips to Morroco, Venezuela, Montreal, and Barbados.

1991 Linda achieves national "Queen of Sales" at Finelle and earns a Lincoln Continental.

1991 Andrew is born.

1991 Brian resigns from his job at Briggs & Stratton.

1992 Fire destroys Linda and Brian's Finelle business office.

1993 Linda earns her second Lincoln Continental from Finelle.

1994 Linda leaves Finelle and along with Brian joins the corporate office team of Viviane Woodard.

1997 Linda and Brian resign their positions at Viviane Woodard.

1998 Linda and Brian launch L'Bri Pure n' Natural.

1999 L'Bri Pure n' Natural moves its offices to Perkins Drive. Sales exceed one million dollars.

2004 Perkins Drive office-warehouse expands to 10,000 square feet.

2007 Sales exceed five million dollars.

MISSION STATEMENT

At L'Bri Pure n' Natural, we are committed to advancing products and opportunities that develop a lifetime of self-confidence while enhancing personal appearance and self-esteem within a supportive and nurturing environment.

We are dedicated to promoting the development of individuals to achieve their fullest potential, enabling them to accomplish whatever they desire, limited only by their own initiative.

We will respect each individual at every level within our organization, and enhance the life of every person we touch.

TO LEARN MORE

To learn more about L'Bri Pure n' Natural, visit the company's website at www.lbri.com.

To request free samples of several of the most popular L'Bri products, contact your independent L'Bri Consultant or log on to www.lbri.net/samples.

ABOUT JIM WALDSMITH

Jim Waldsmith is a professional writer who works with Fortune 500 companies and executives. A former news reporter, editor, and news director, this award-winning journalist is an accomplished speechwriter and producer. His company, Jim Waldsmith's Creative Arts, LLC, produces conventions and video projects throughout the United States and in Europe. Jim can be reached at www.jwca.com.